WEEDINO

GENEVIÈVE LEBLEU

D1072930

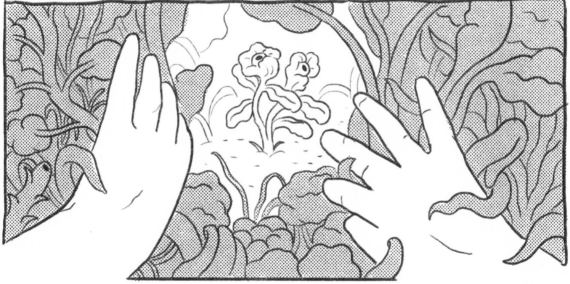
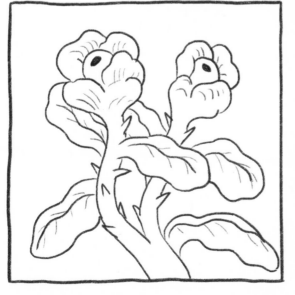
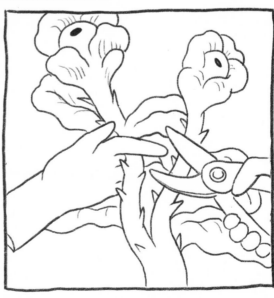

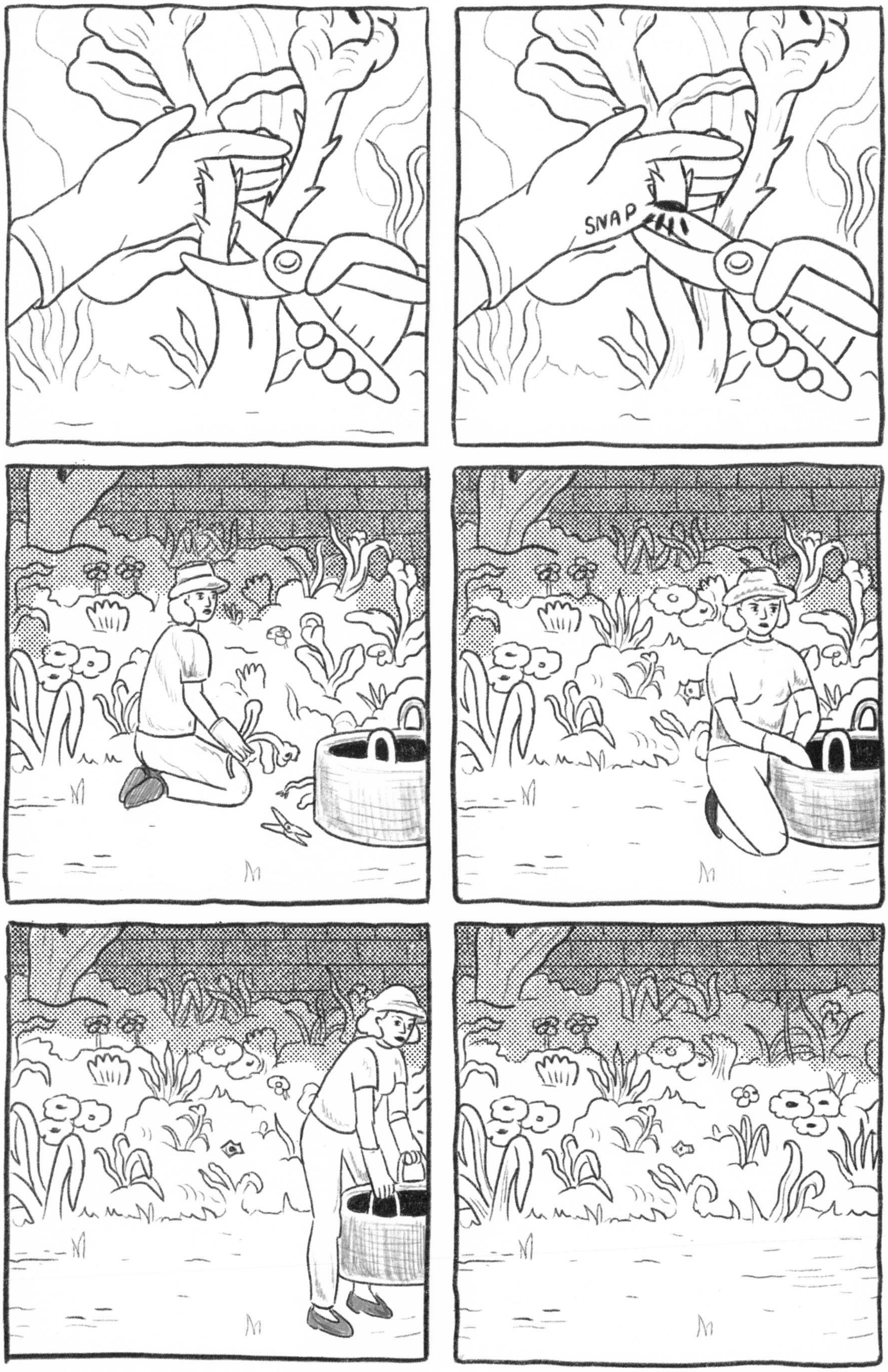
SNAP

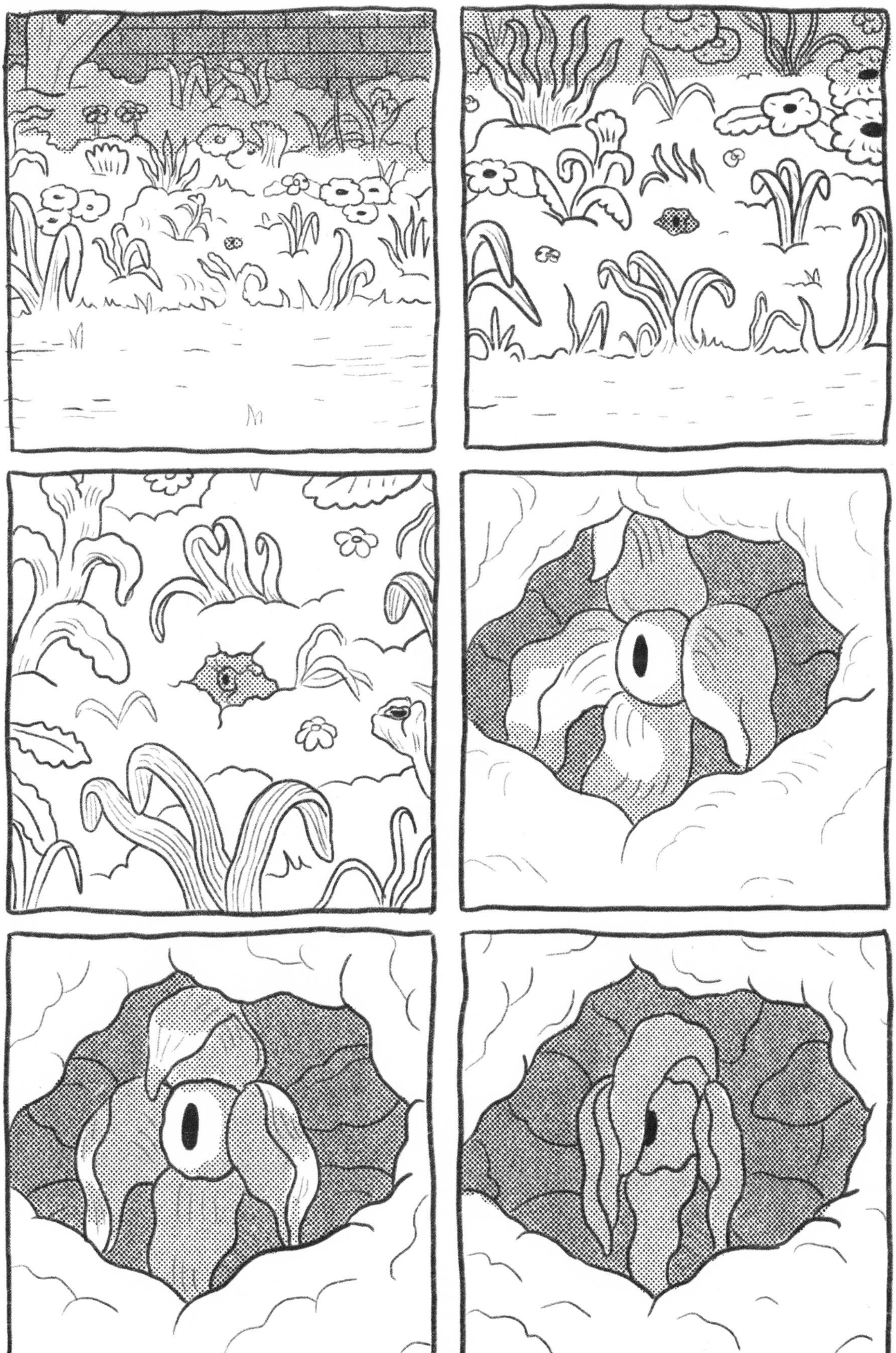

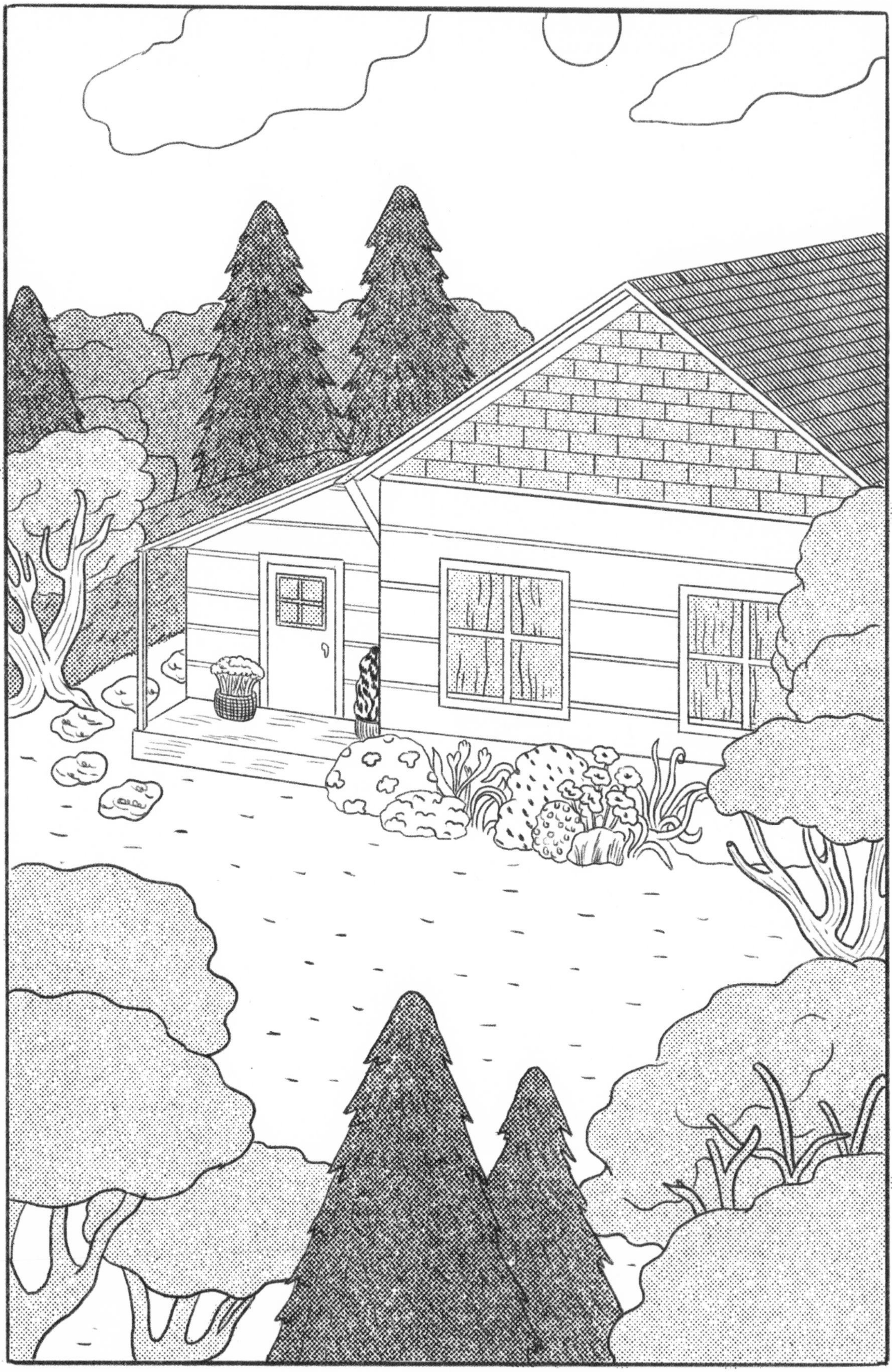

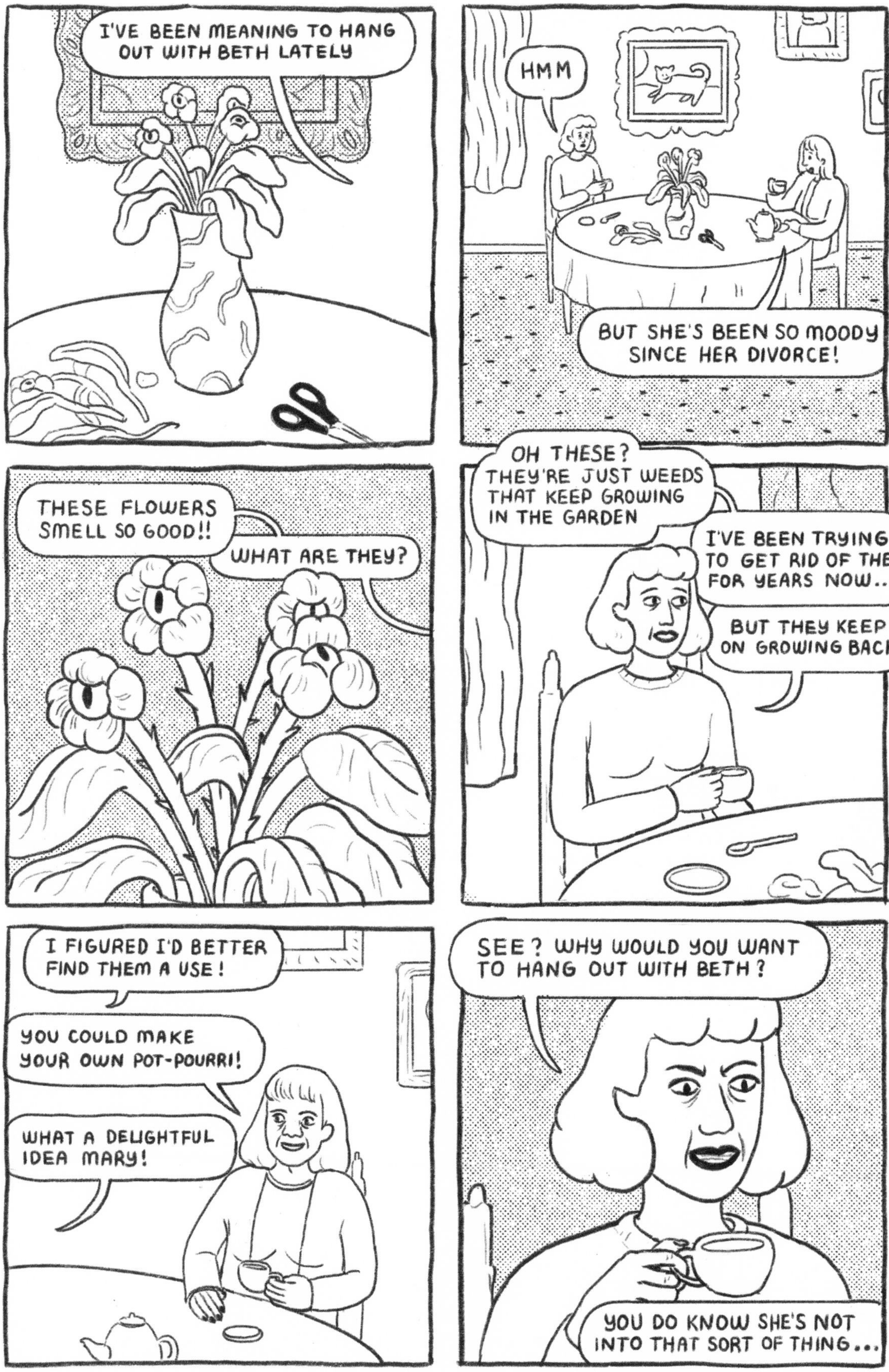
I'VE BEEN MEANING TO HANG OUT WITH BETH LATELY
HMM
BUT SHE'S BEEN SO MOODY SINCE HER DIVORCE!
THESE FLOWERS SMELL SO GOOD!!
WHAT ARE THEY?
OH THESE? THEY'RE JUST WEEDS THAT KEEP GROWING IN THE GARDEN
I'VE BEEN TRYING TO GET RID OF THEM FOR YEARS NOW...
BUT THEY KEEP ON GROWING BACK
I FIGURED I'D BETTER FIND THEM A USE!
YOU COULD MAKE YOUR OWN POT-POURRI!
WHAT A DELIGHTFUL IDEA MARY!
SEE? WHY WOULD YOU WANT TO HANG OUT WITH BETH?
YOU DO KNOW SHE'S NOT INTO THAT SORT OF THING...

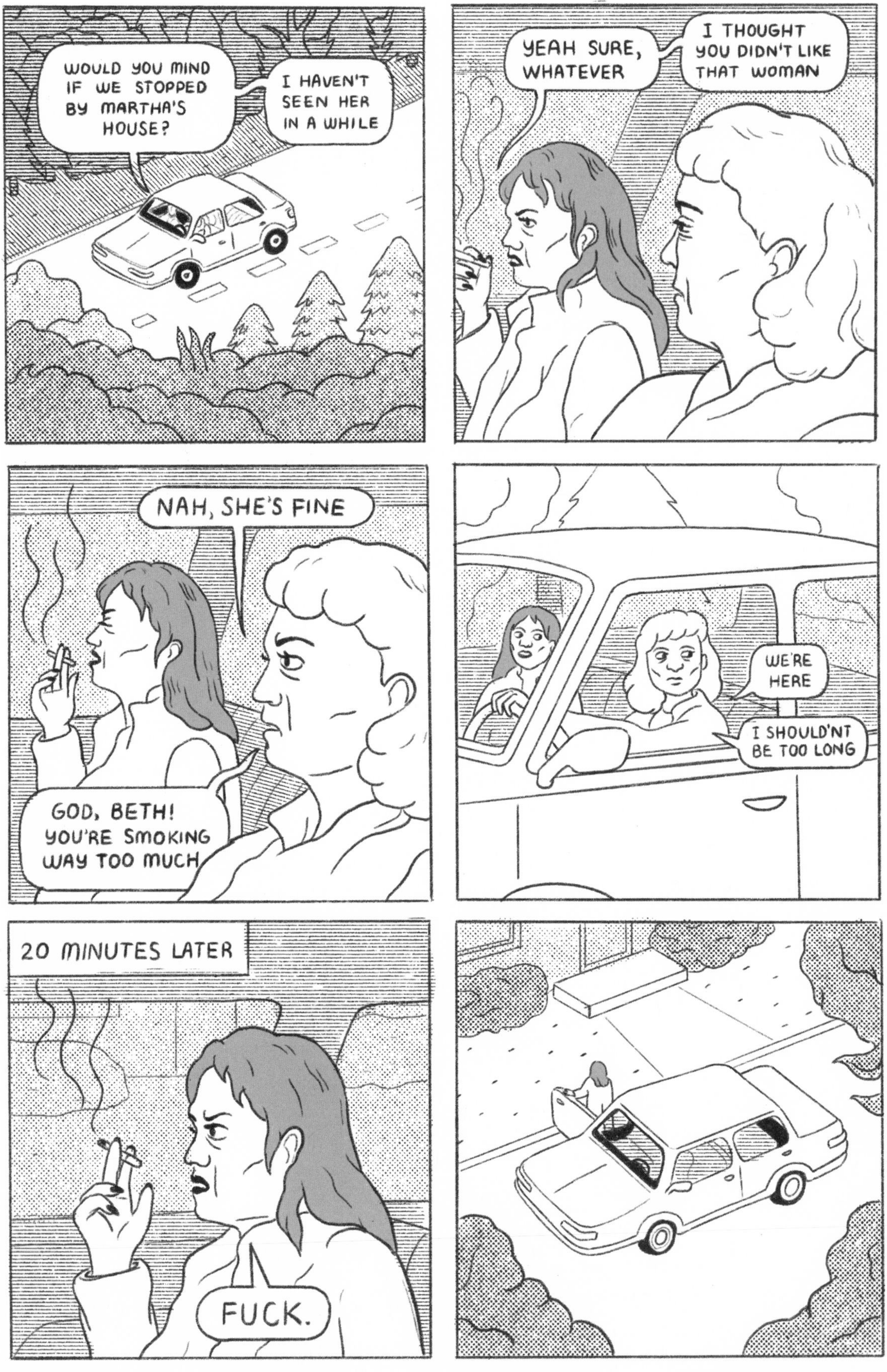
WOULD YOU MIND IF WE STOPPED BY MARTHA'S HOUSE?
I HAVEN'T SEEN HER IN A WHILE
YEAH SURE, WHATEVER
I THOUGHT YOU DIDN'T LIKE THAT WOMAN
NAH, SHE'S FINE
GOD, BETH! YOU'RE SMOKING WAY TOO MUCH
WE'RE HERE
I SHOULD'NT BE TOO LONG
20 MINUTES LATER
FUCK.

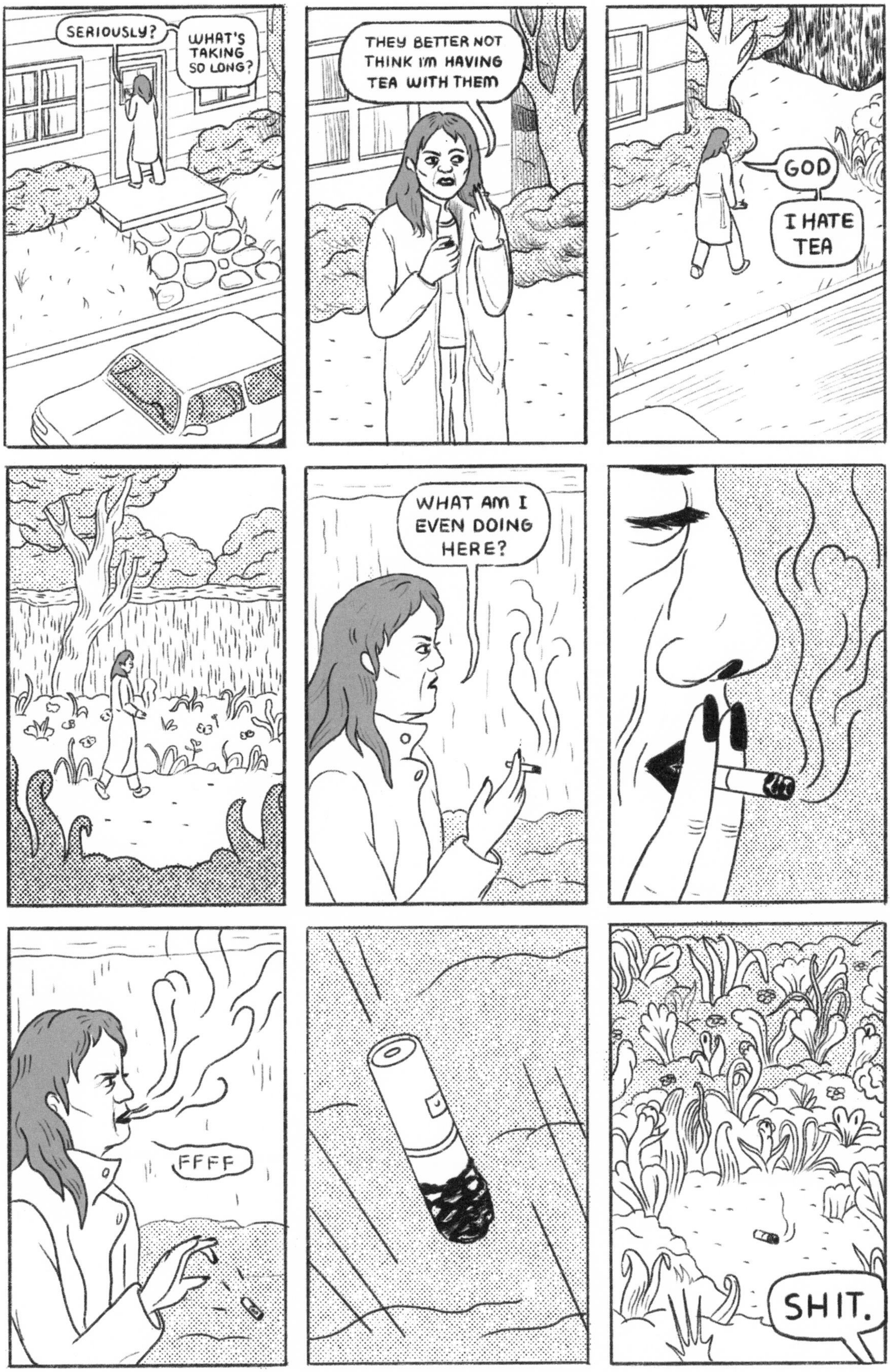
SERIOUSLY?
WHAT'S TAKING SO LONG?
THEY BETTER NOT THINK I'M HAVING TEA WITH THEM
GOD
I HATE TEA
WHAT AM I EVEN DOING HERE?
FFFF
SHIT.

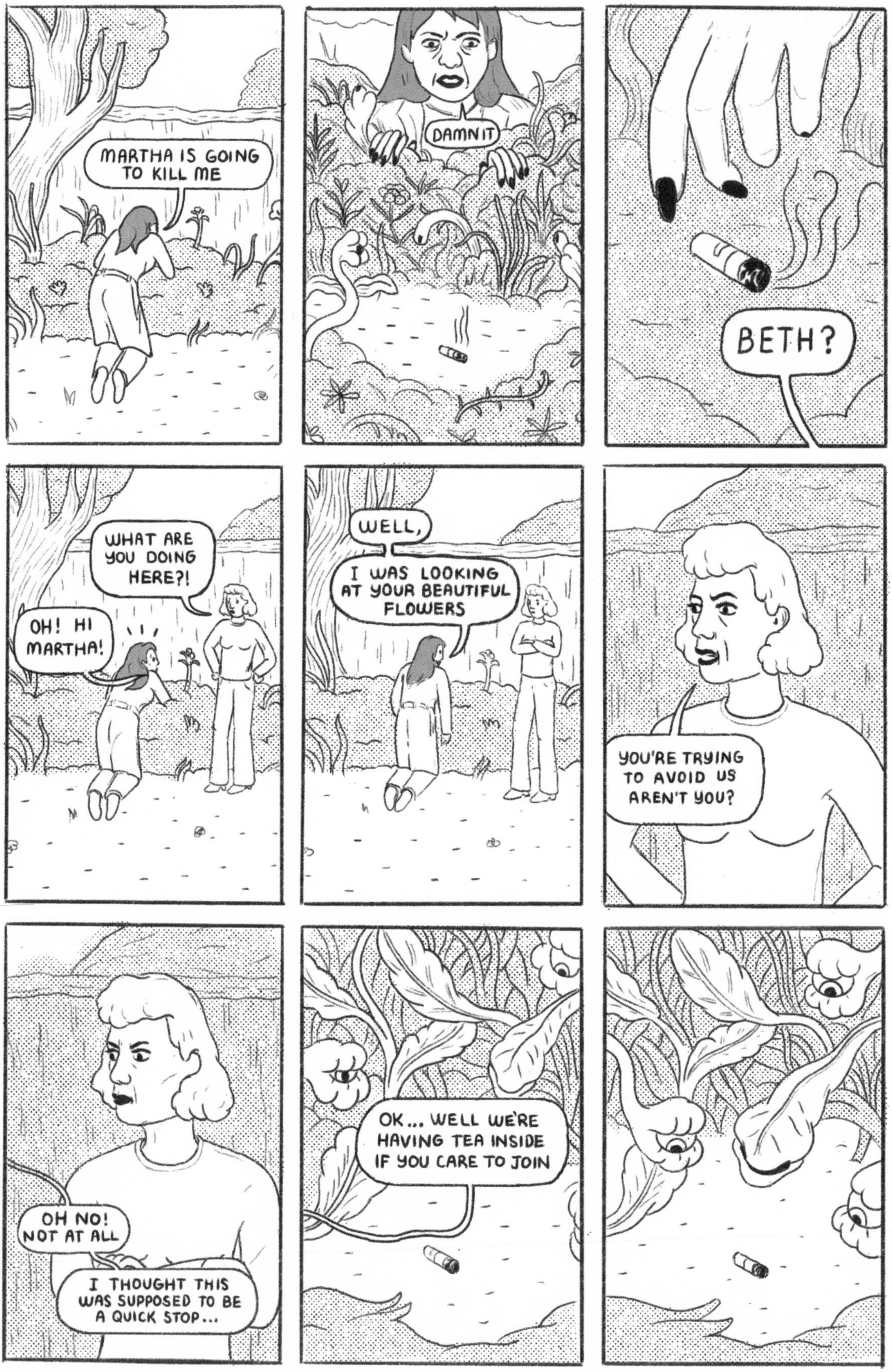
MARTHA IS GOING TO KILL ME
DAMNIT
BETH?
WHAT ARE YOU DOING HERE?!
OH! HI MARTHA!
WELL,
I WAS LOOKING AT YOUR BEAUTIFUL FLOWERS
YOU'RE TRYING TO AVOID US AREN'T YOU?
OH NO! NOT AT ALL
I THOUGHT THIS WAS SUPPOSED TO BE A QUICK STOP...
OK... WELL WE'RE HAVING TEA INSIDE IF YOU CARE TO JOIN

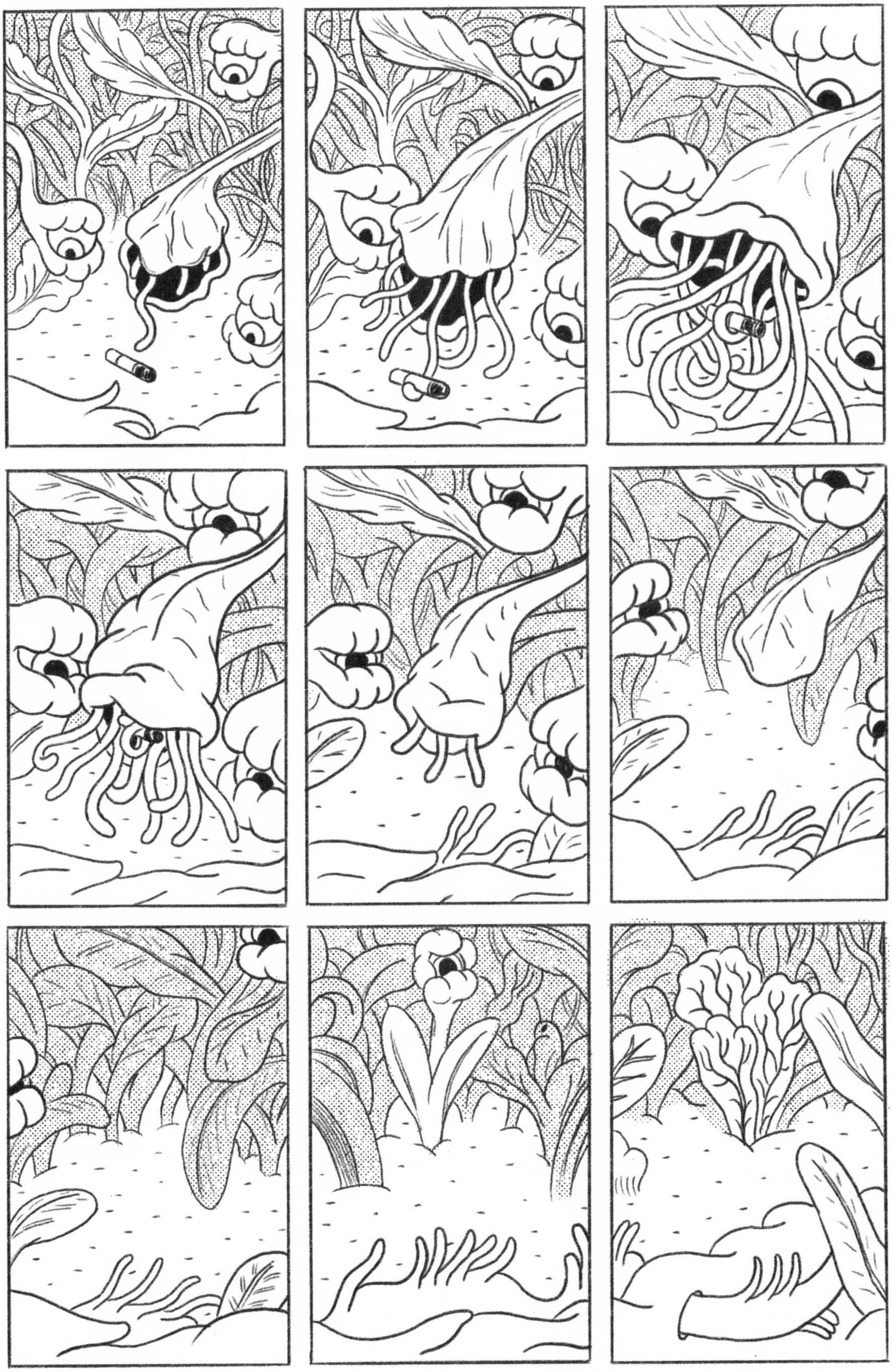

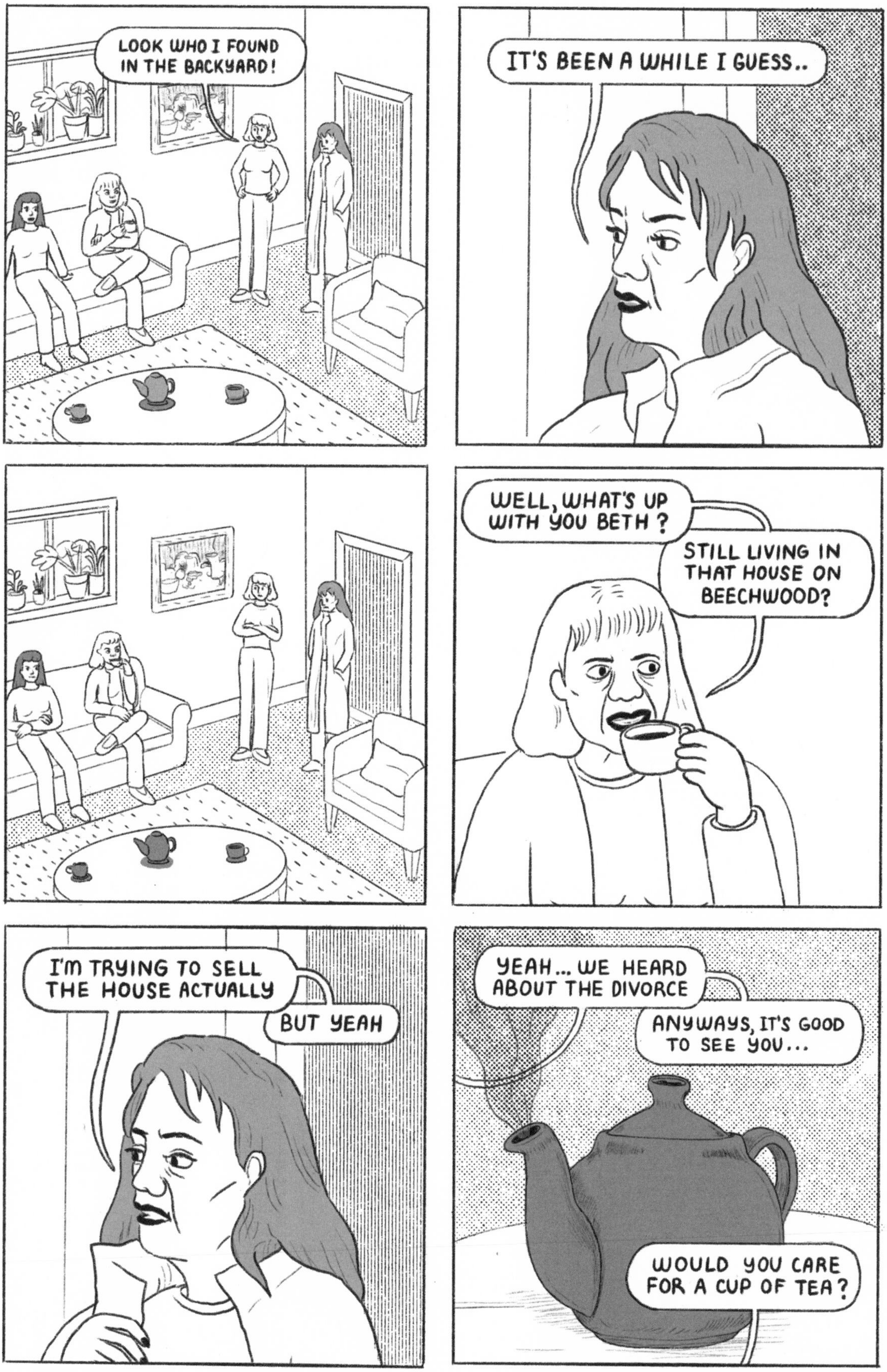
LOOK WHO I FOUND IN THE BACKYARD!
IT'S BEEN A WHILE I GUESS..
WELL, WHAT'S UP WITH YOU BETH?
STILL LIVING IN THAT HOUSE ON BEECHWOOD?
I'M TRYING TO SELL THE HOUSE ACTUALLY
BUT YEAH
YEAH... WE HEARD ABOUT THE DIVORCE
ANYWAYS, IT'S GOOD TO SEE YOU...
WOULD YOU CARE FOR A CUP OF TEA?

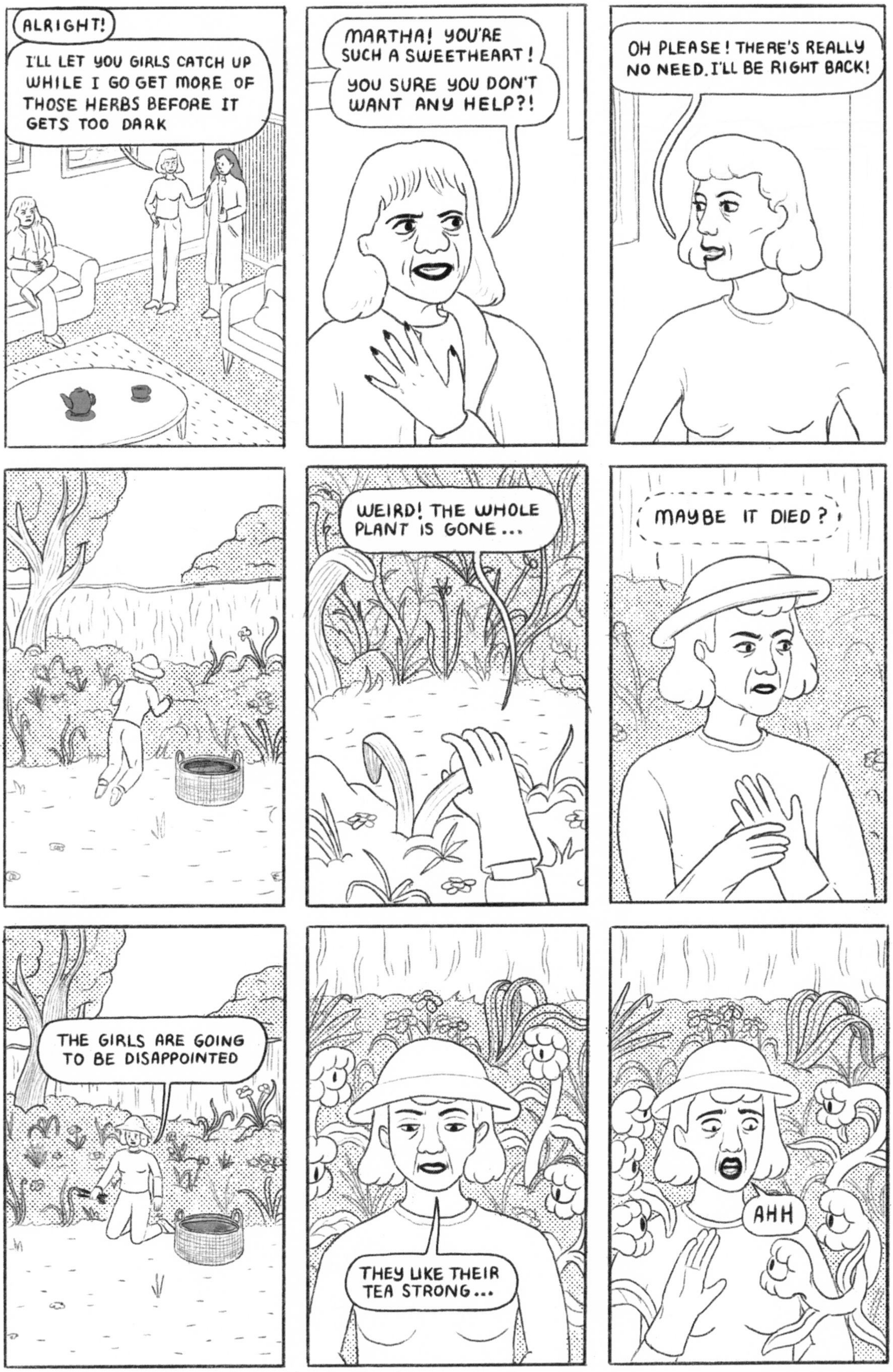
ALRIGHT!
I'LL LET YOU GIRLS CATCH UP WHILE I GO GET MORE OF THOSE HERBS BEFORE IT GETS TOO DARK
MARTHA! YOU'RE SUCH A SWEETHEART!
YOU SURE YOU DON'T WANT ANY HELP?!
OH PLEASE! THERE'S REALLY NO NEED. I'LL BE RIGHT BACK!
WEIRD! THE WHOLE PLANT IS GONE...
MAYBE IT DIED?
THE GIRLS ARE GOING TO BE DISAPPOINTED
THEY LIKE THEIR TEA STRONG...
AHH

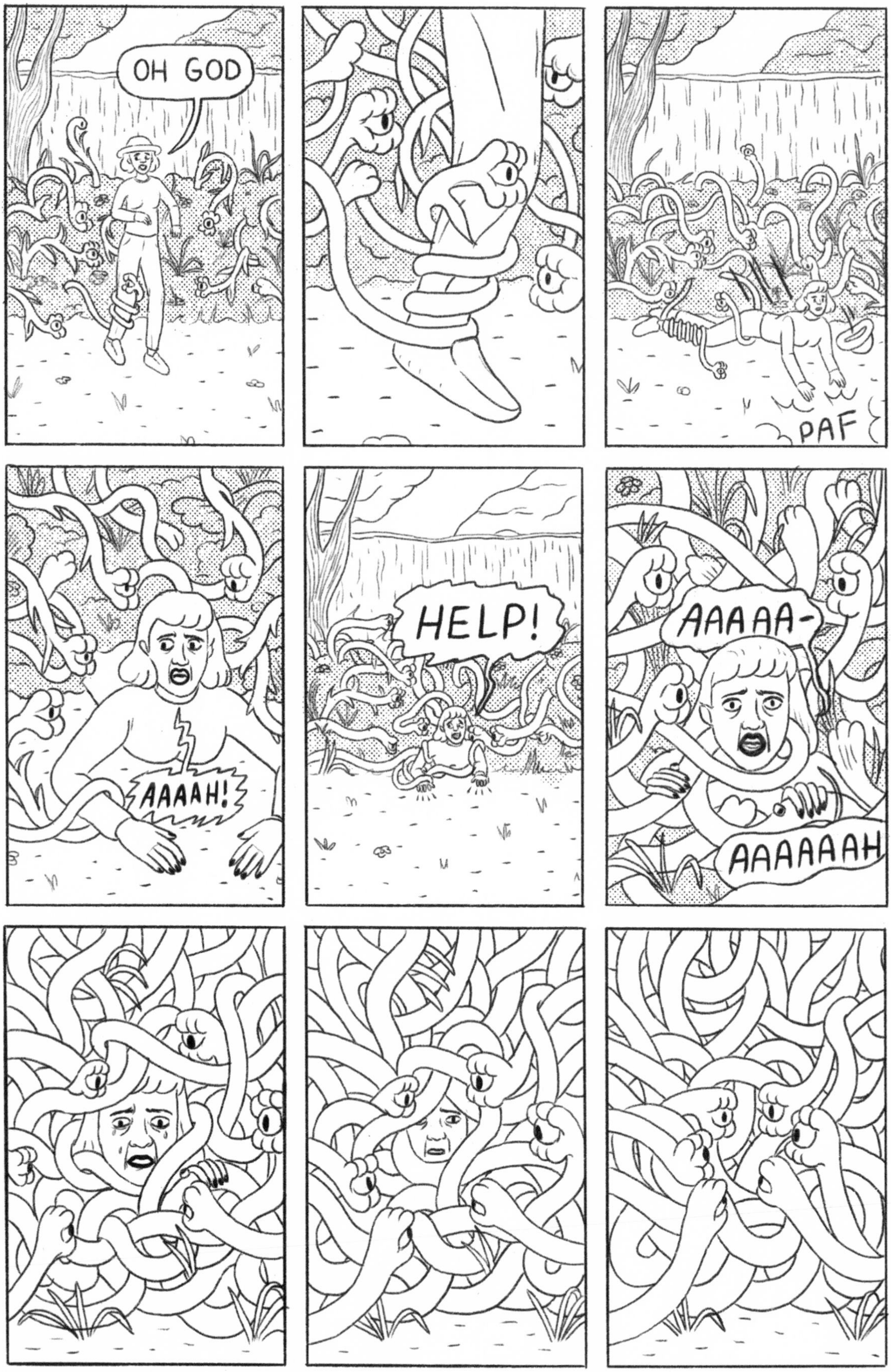
OH GOD
PAF
AAAAH!
HELP!
AAAAA-
AAAAAAH

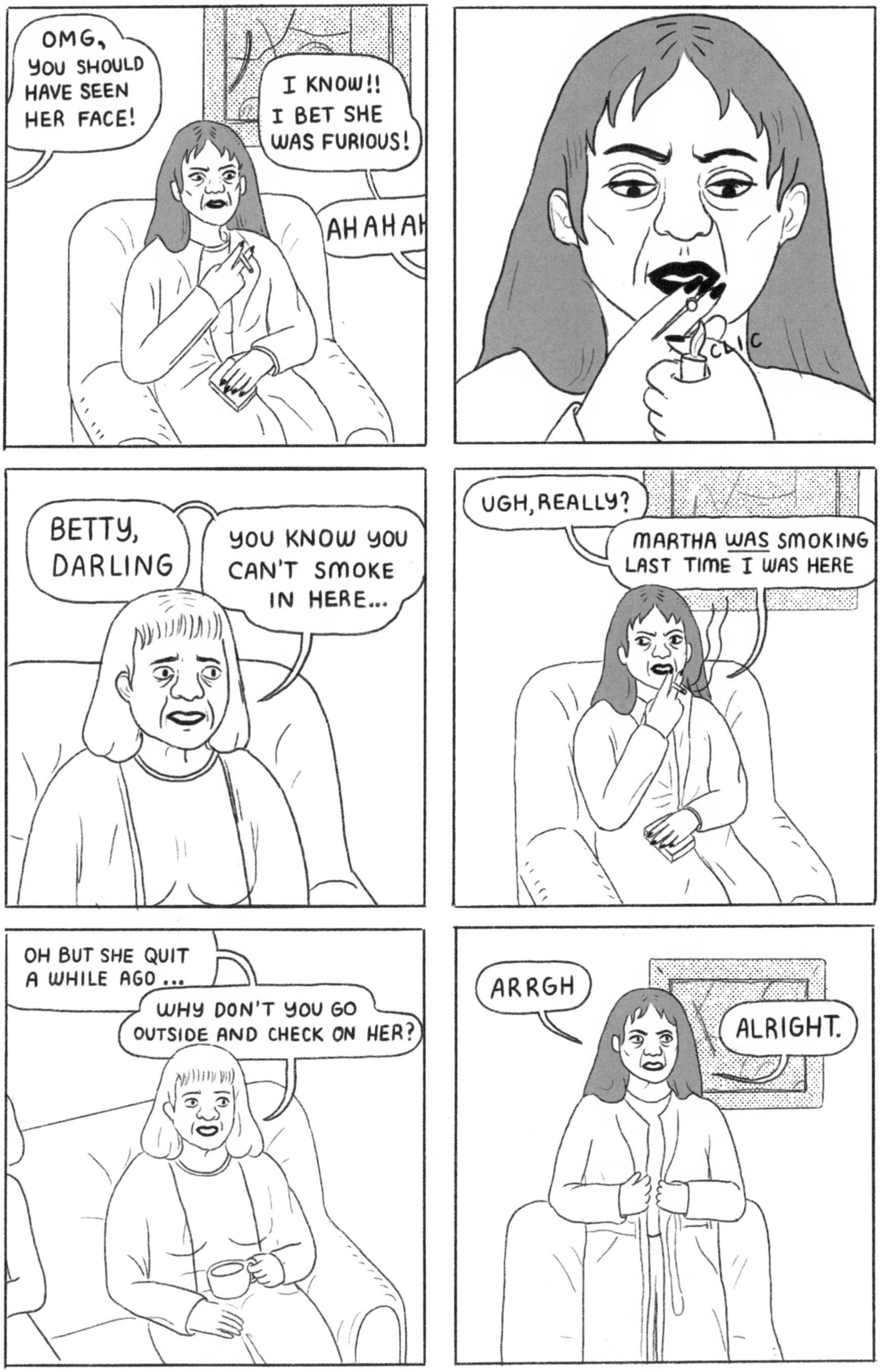
OMG, YOU SHOULD HAVE SEEN HER FACE!
I KNOW!! I BET SHE WAS FURIOUS!
AHAHAH
CLIC
BETTY, DARLING
YOU KNOW YOU CAN'T SMOKE IN HERE...
UGH, REALLY?
MARTHA WAS SMOKING LAST TIME I WAS HERE
OH BUT SHE QUIT A WHILE AGO ...
WHY DON'T YOU GO OUTSIDE AND CHECK ON HER?
ARRGH
ALRIGHT.

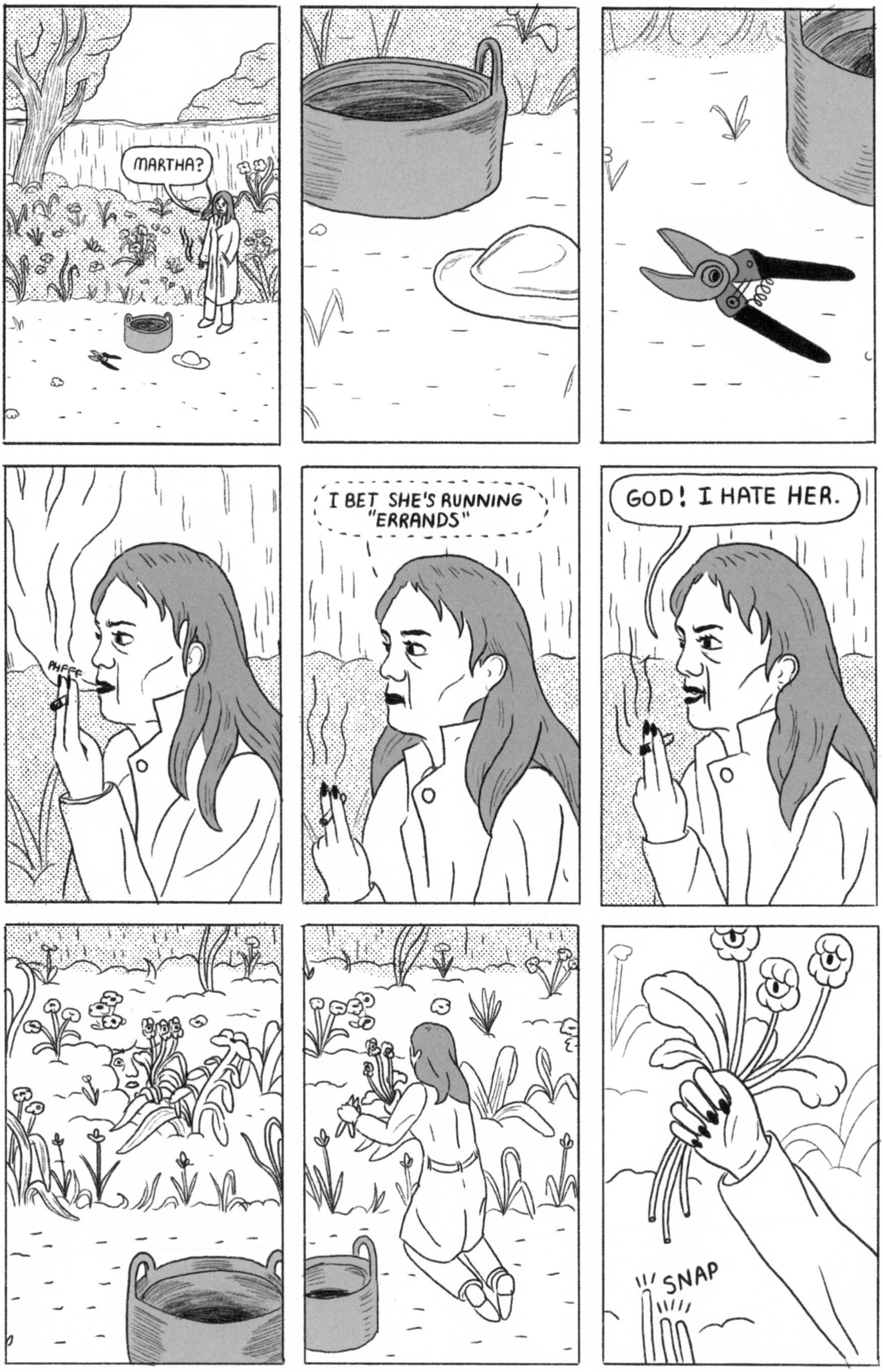
MARTHA?
PHFFF
I BET SHE'S RUNNING "ERRANDS"
GOD! I HATE HER.
SNAP

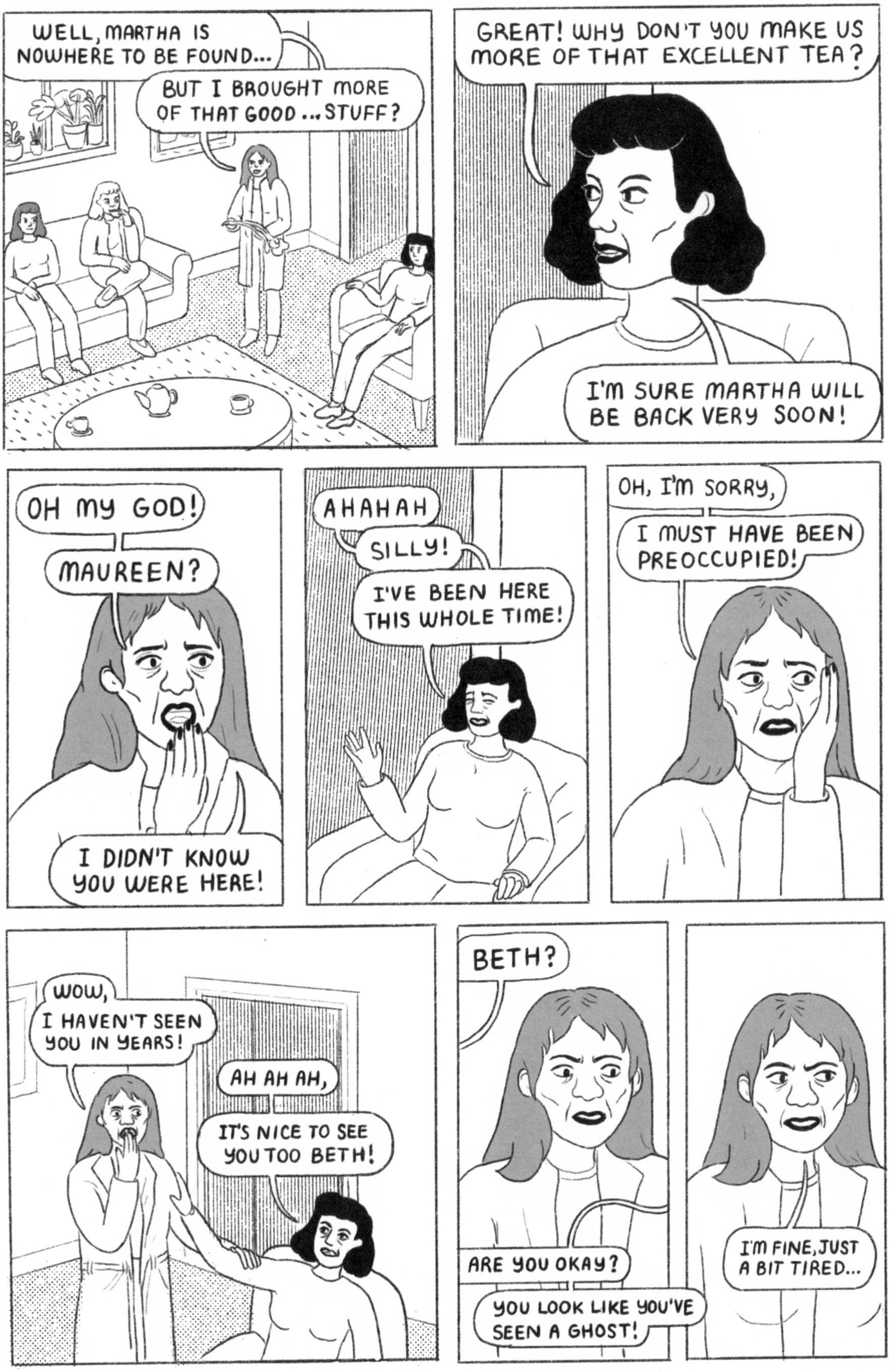
WELL, MARTHA IS NOWHERE TO BE FOUND...
BUT I BROUGHT MORE OF THAT GOOD ... STUFF?
GREAT! WHY DON'T YOU MAKE US MORE OF THAT EXCELLENT TEA?
I'M SURE MARTHA WILL BE BACK VERY SOON!
OH MY GOD!
MAUREEN?
I DIDN'T KNOW YOU WERE HERE!
AHAHAH
SILLY!
I'VE BEEN HERE THIS WHOLE TIME!
OH, I'M SORRY,
I MUST HAVE BEEN PREOCCUPIED!
WOW,
I HAVEN'T SEEN YOU IN YEARS!
AH AH AH,
IT'S NICE TO SEE YOU TOO BETH!
BETH?
ARE YOU OKAY?
YOU LOOK LIKE YOU'VE SEEN A GHOST!
I'M FINE, JUST A BIT TIRED...

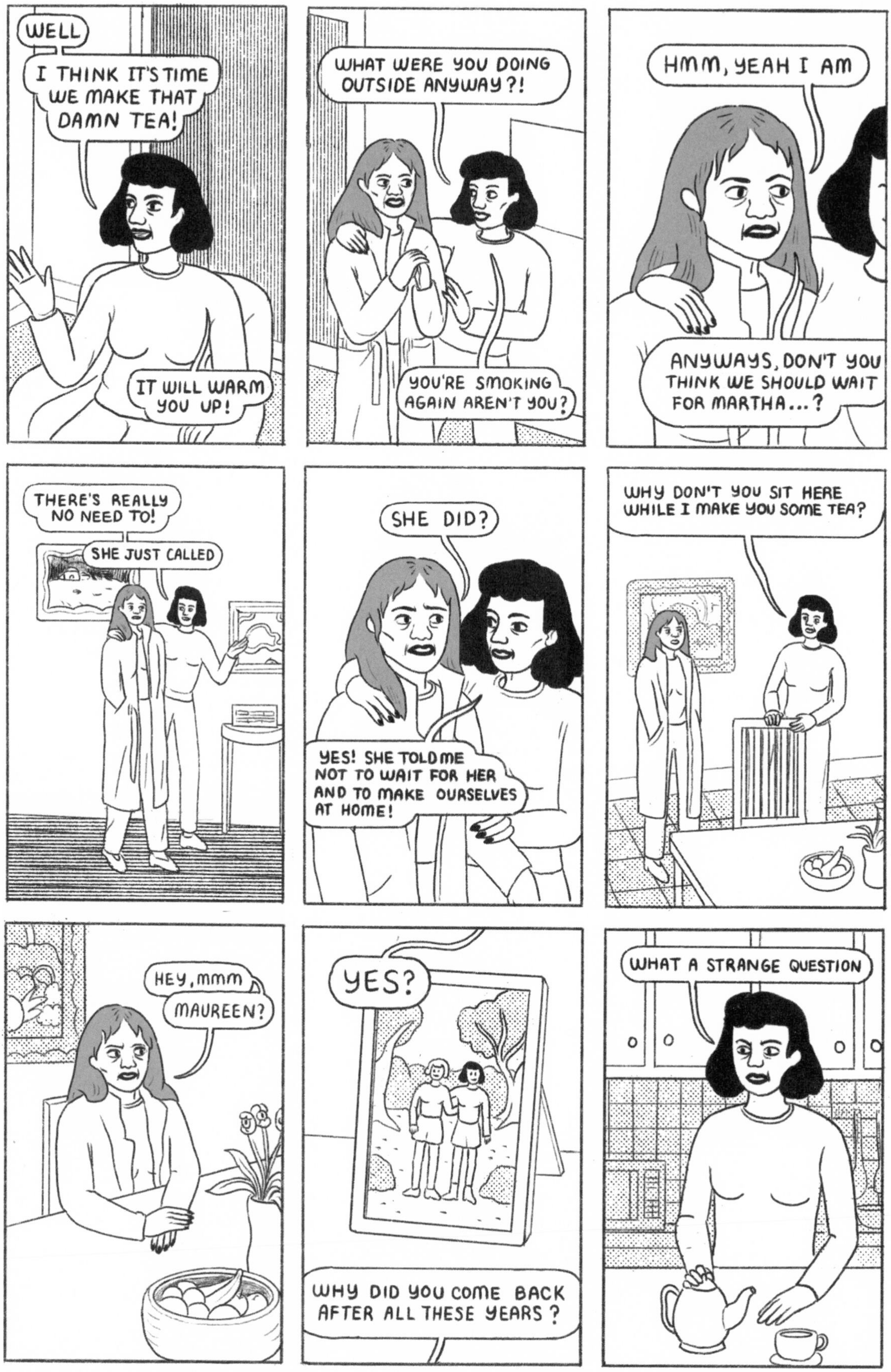
WELL
I THINK IT'S TIME WE MAKE THAT DAMN TEA!
IT WILL WARM YOU UP!
WHAT WERE YOU DOING OUTSIDE ANYWAY?!
YOU'RE SMOKING AGAIN AREN'T YOU?
HMM, YEAH I AM
ANYWAYS, DON'T YOU THINK WE SHOULD WAIT FOR MARTHA...?
THERE'S REALLY NO NEED TO!
SHE JUST CALLED
SHE DID?
YES! SHE TOLD ME NOT TO WAIT FOR HER AND TO MAKE OURSELVES AT HOME!
WHY DON'T YOU SIT HERE WHILE I MAKE YOU SOME TEA?
HEY, mmm
MAUREEN?
YES?
WHY DID YOU COME BACK AFTER ALL THESE YEARS?
WHAT A STRANGE QUESTION

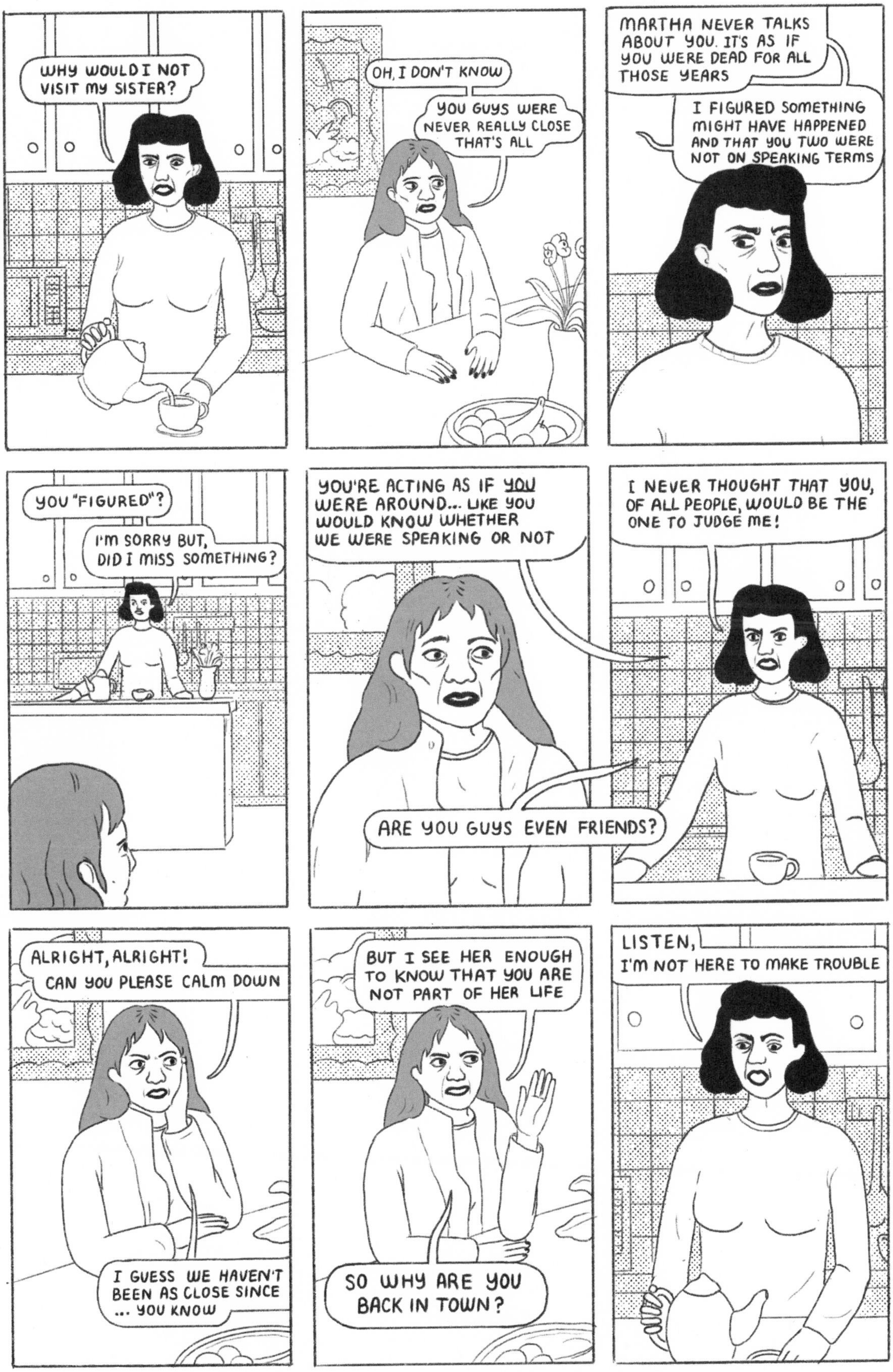
WHY WOULD I NOT VISIT MY SISTER?
OH, I DON'T KNOW
YOU GUYS WERE NEVER REALLY CLOSE THAT'S ALL
MARTHA NEVER TALKS ABOUT YOU. IT'S AS IF YOU WERE DEAD FOR ALL THOSE YEARS
I FIGURED SOMETHING MIGHT HAVE HAPPENED AND THAT YOU TWO WERE NOT ON SPEAKING TERMS
YOU "FIGURED"?
I'M SORRY BUT, DID I MISS SOMETHING?
YOU'RE ACTING AS IF YOU WERE AROUND... LIKE YOU WOULD KNOW WHETHER WE WERE SPEAKING OR NOT
ARE YOU GUYS EVEN FRIENDS?
I NEVER THOUGHT THAT YOU, OF ALL PEOPLE, WOULD BE THE ONE TO JUDGE ME!
ALRIGHT, ALRIGHT!
CAN YOU PLEASE CALM DOWN
I GUESS WE HAVEN'T BEEN AS CLOSE SINCE ... YOU KNOW
BUT I SEE HER ENOUGH TO KNOW THAT YOU ARE NOT PART OF HER LIFE
SO WHY ARE YOU BACK IN TOWN?
LISTEN,
I'M NOT HERE TO MAKE TROUBLE

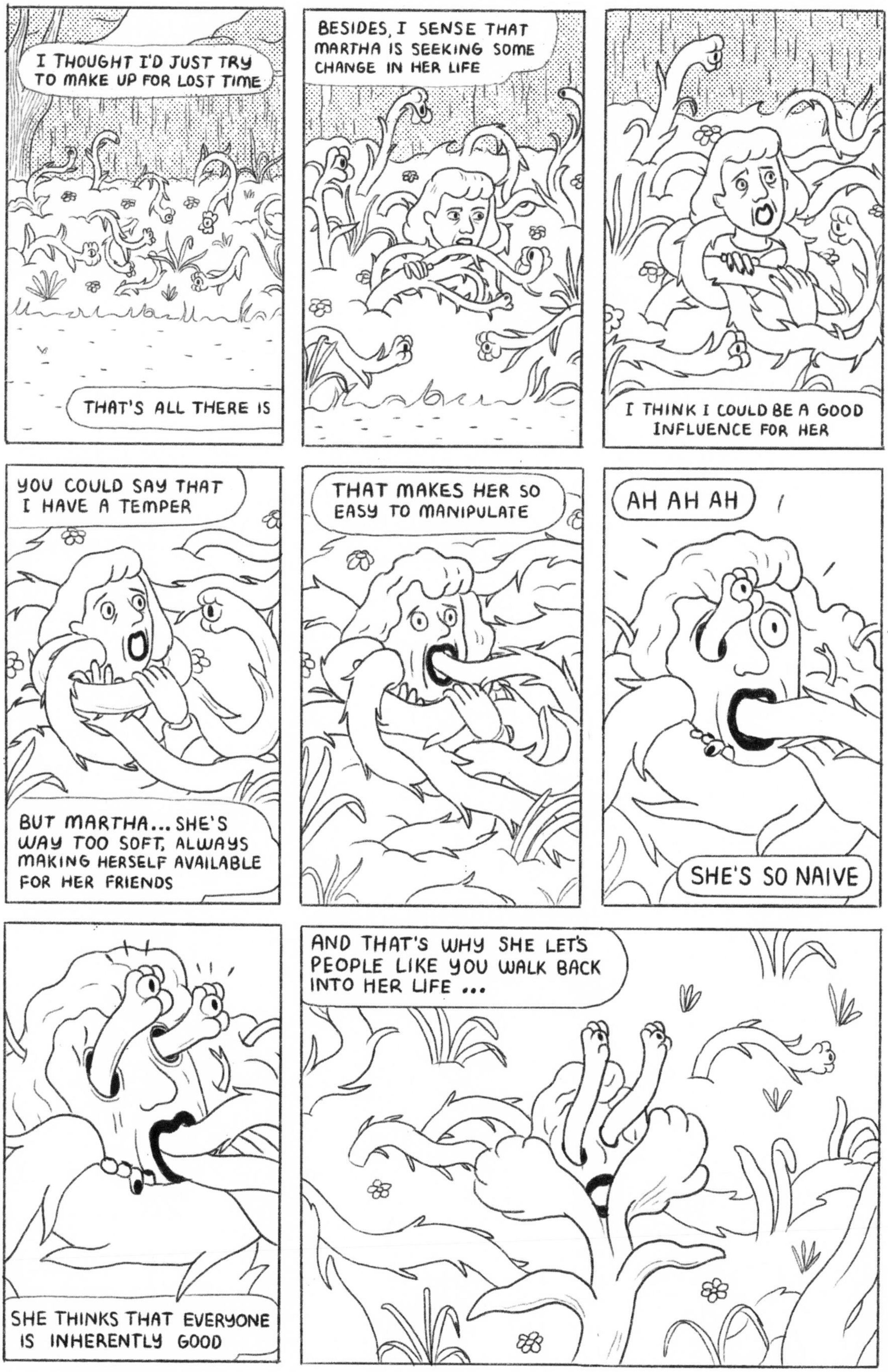
I THOUGHT I'D JUST TRY TO MAKE UP FOR LOST TIME
THAT'S ALL THERE IS
BESIDES, I SENSE THAT MARTHA IS SEEKING SOME CHANGE IN HER LIFE
I THINK I COULD BE A GOOD INFLUENCE FOR HER
YOU COULD SAY THAT I HAVE A TEMPER
BUT MARTHA... SHE'S WAY TOO SOFT, ALWAYS MAKING HERSELF AVAILABLE FOR HER FRIENDS
THAT MAKES HER SO EASY TO MANIPULATE
AH AH AH
SHE'S SO NAIVE
SHE THINKS THAT EVERYONE IS INHERENTLY GOOD
AND THAT'S WHY SHE LET'S PEOPLE LIKE YOU WALK BACK INTO HER LIFE ...

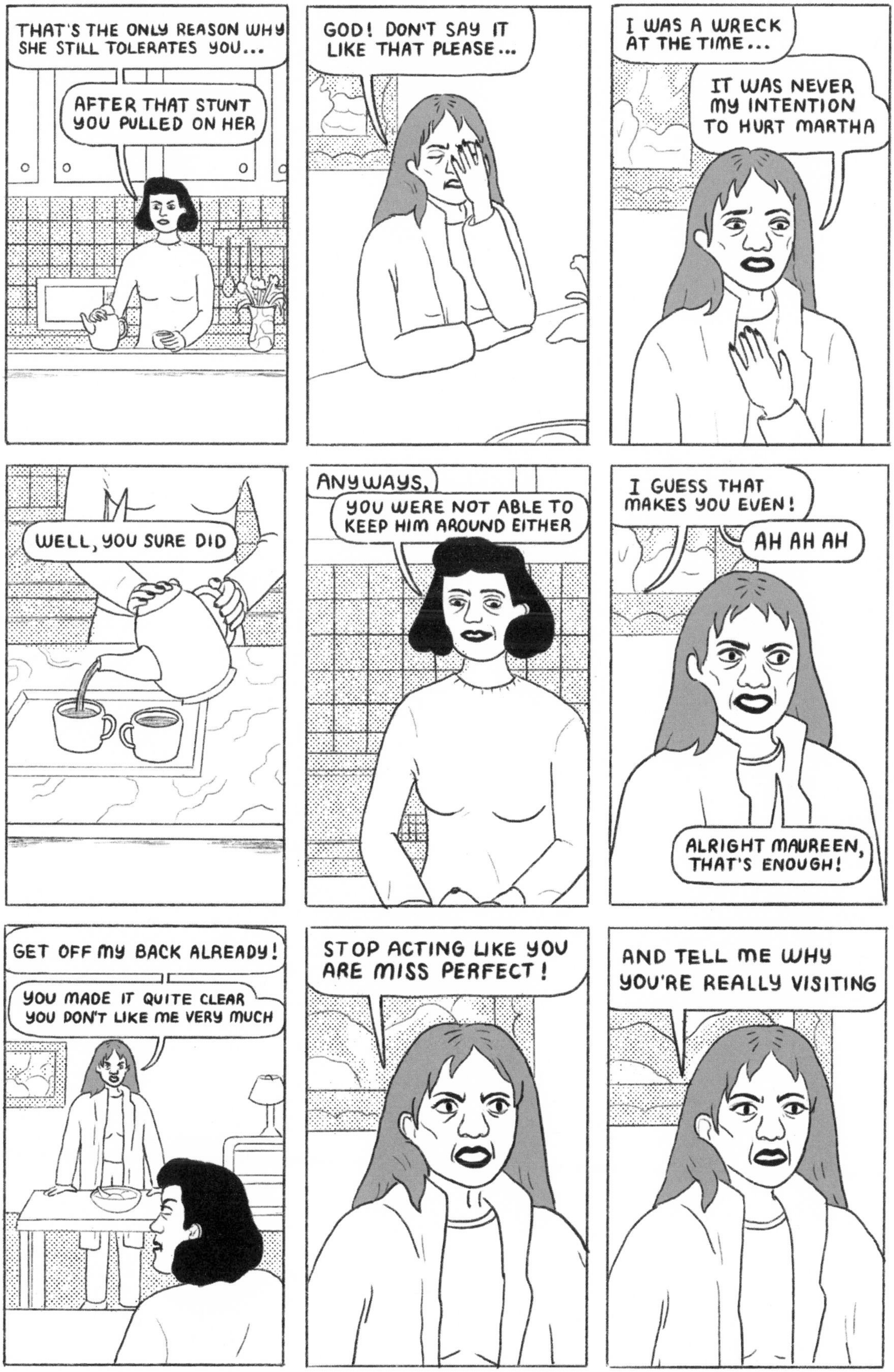
THAT'S THE ONLY REASON WHY SHE STILL TOLERATES YOU...
AFTER THAT STUNT YOU PULLED ON HER
GOD! DON'T SAY IT LIKE THAT PLEASE...
I WAS A WRECK AT THE TIME...
IT WAS NEVER MY INTENTION TO HURT MARTHA
WELL, YOU SURE DID
ANYWAYS,
YOU WERE NOT ABLE TO KEEP HIM AROUND EITHER
I GUESS THAT MAKES YOU EVEN!
AH AH AH
ALRIGHT MAUREEN, THAT'S ENOUGH!
GET OFF MY BACK ALREADY!
YOU MADE IT QUITE CLEAR YOU DON'T LIKE ME VERY MUCH
STOP ACTING LIKE YOU ARE MISS PERFECT!
AND TELL ME WHY YOU'RE REALLY VISITING

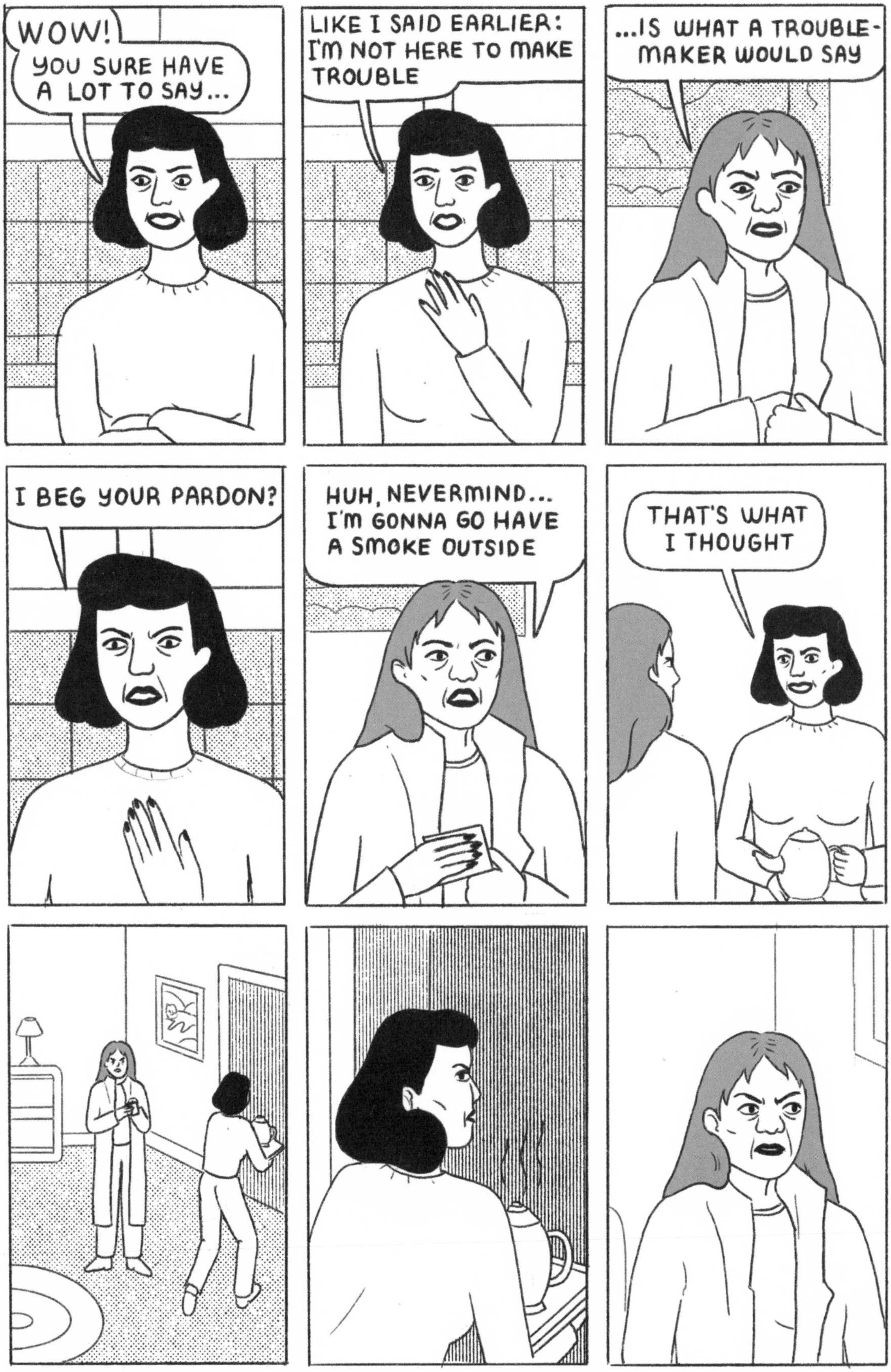
WOW!
YOU SURE HAVE A LOT TO SAY...
LIKE I SAID EARLIER: I'M NOT HERE TO MAKE TROUBLE
...IS WHAT A TROUBLE-MAKER WOULD SAY
I BEG YOUR PARDON?
HUH, NEVERMIND... I'M GONNA GO HAVE A SMOKE OUTSIDE
THAT'S WHAT I THOUGHT

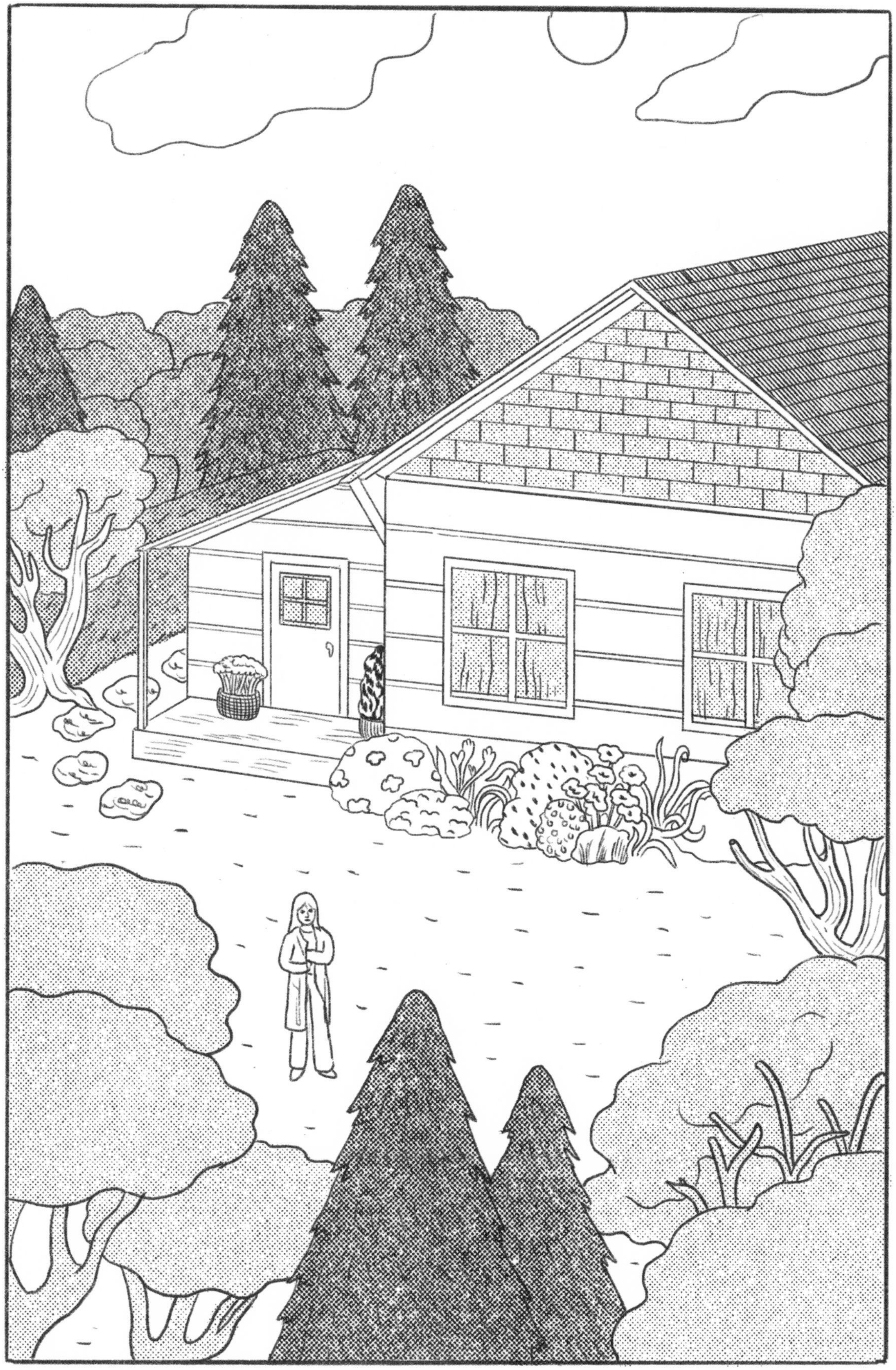

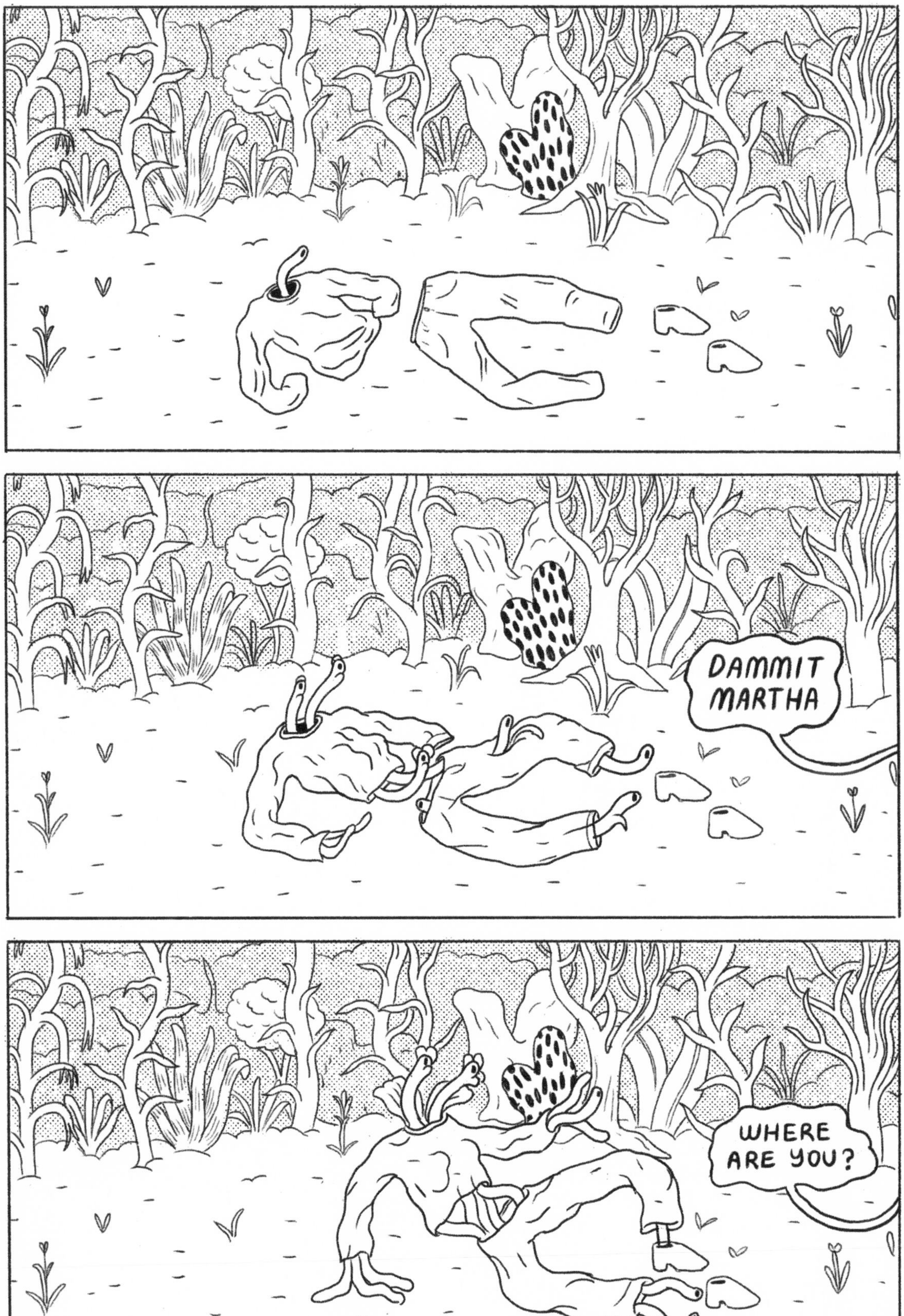
DAMMIT MARTHA
WHERE ARE YOU?

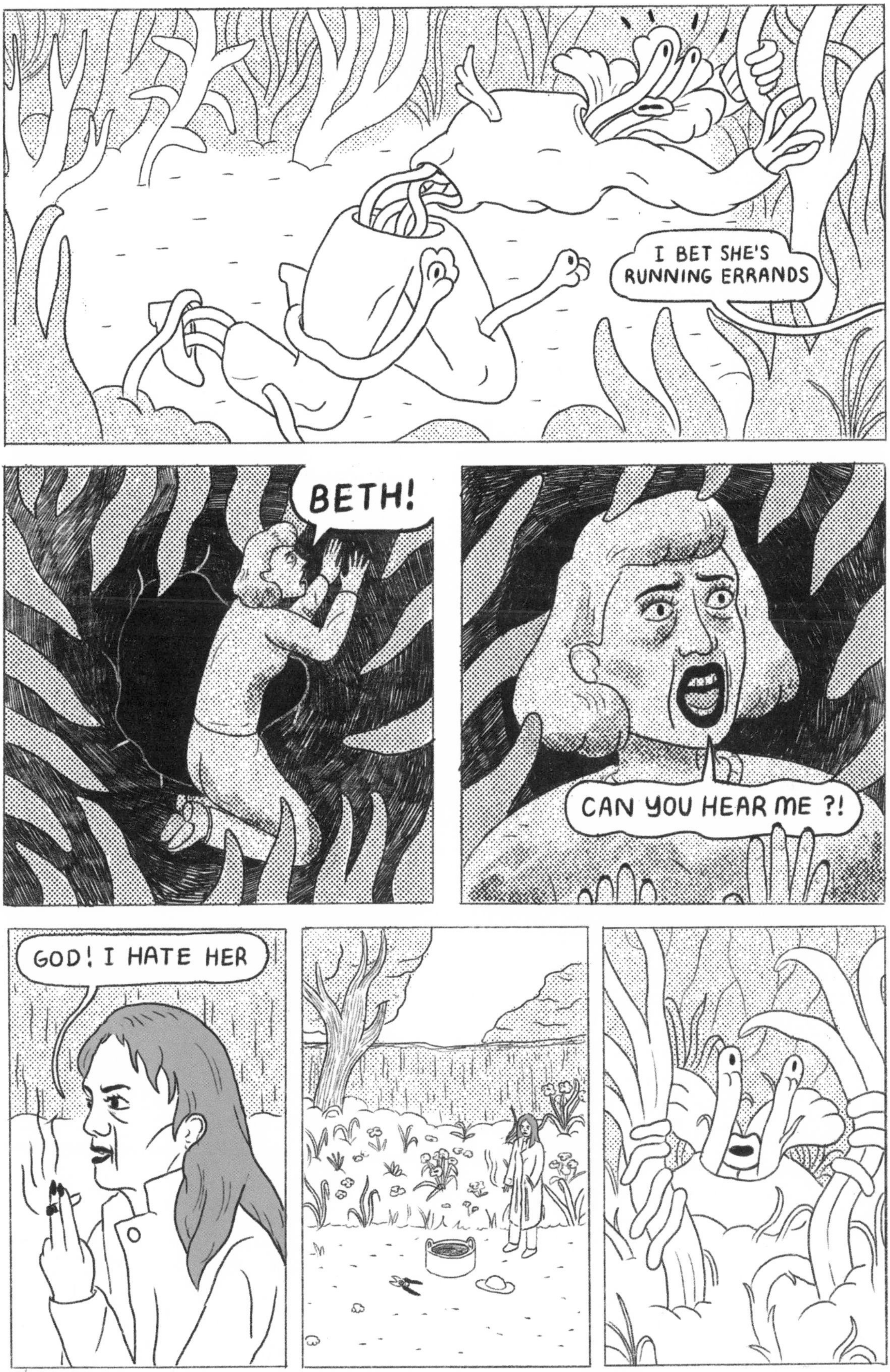

I BET SHE'S RUNNING ERRANDS
BETH!
CAN YOU HEAR ME ?!
GOD! I HATE HER

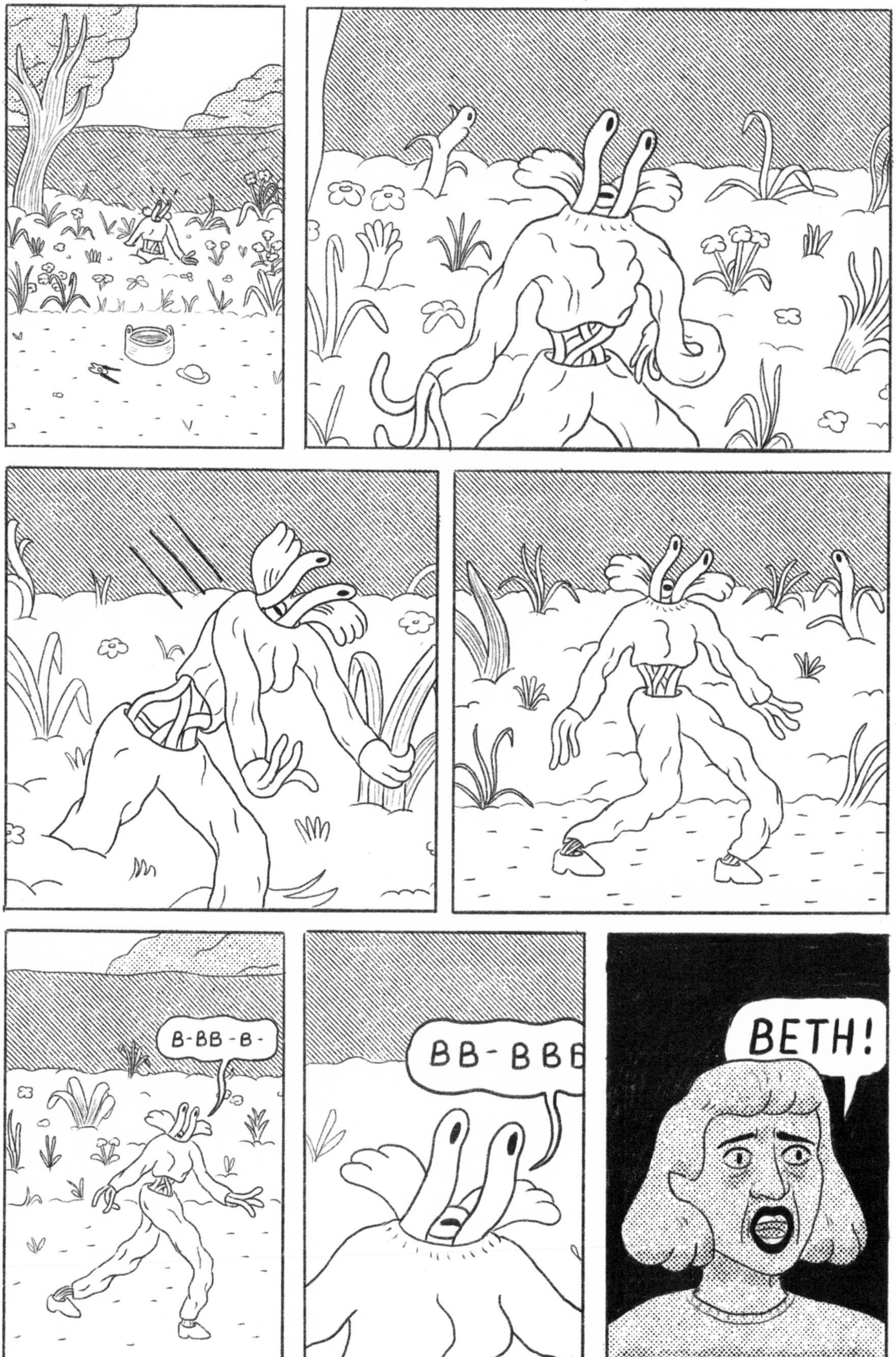
B-BB-B-
BB-BBB
BETH!

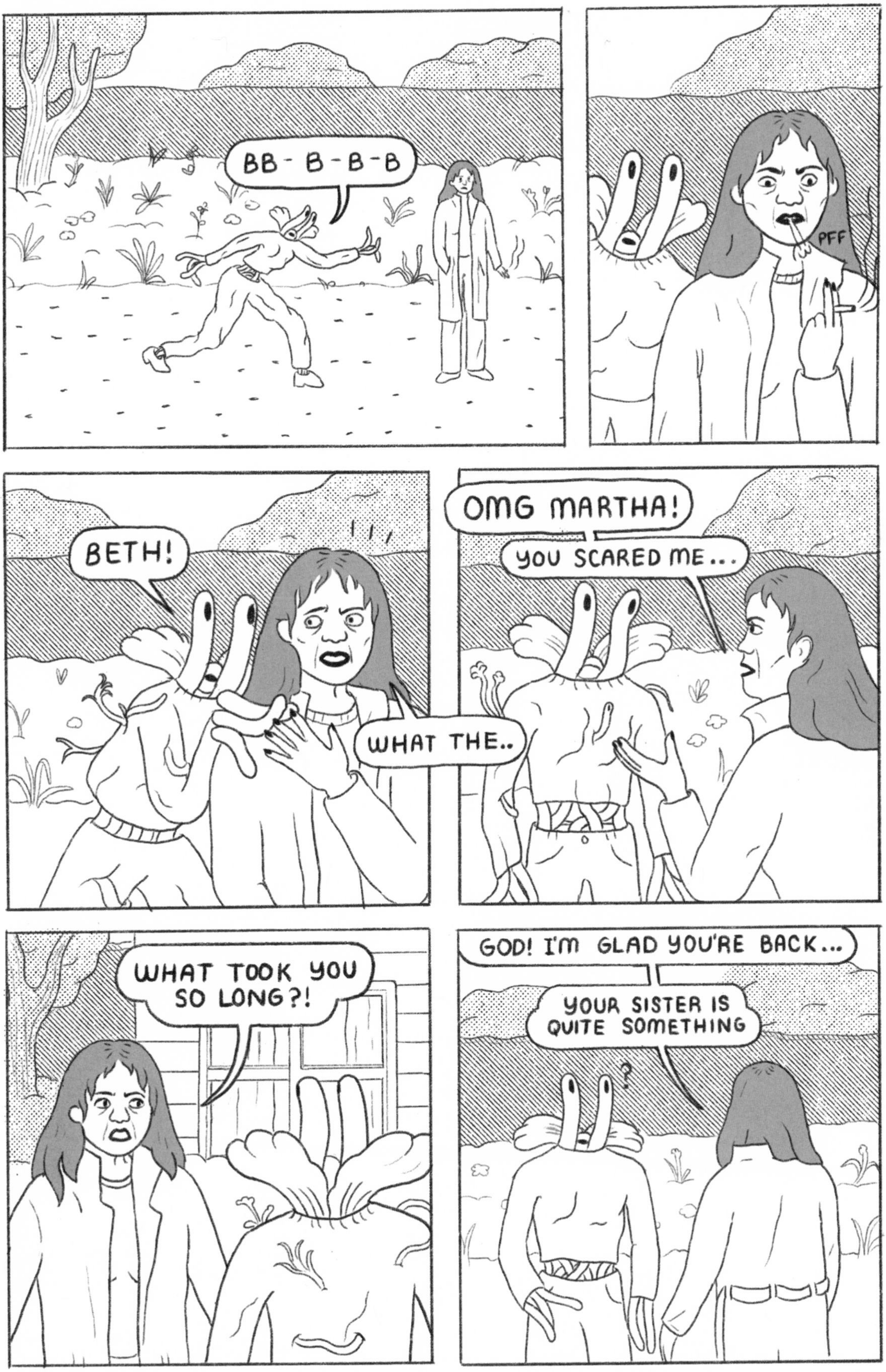
BB-B-B-B
PFF
BETH!
WHAT THE..
OMG MARTHA!
YOU SCARED ME...
WHAT TOOK YOU SO LONG?!
GOD! I'M GLAD YOU'RE BACK...
YOUR SISTER IS QUITE SOMETHING
?

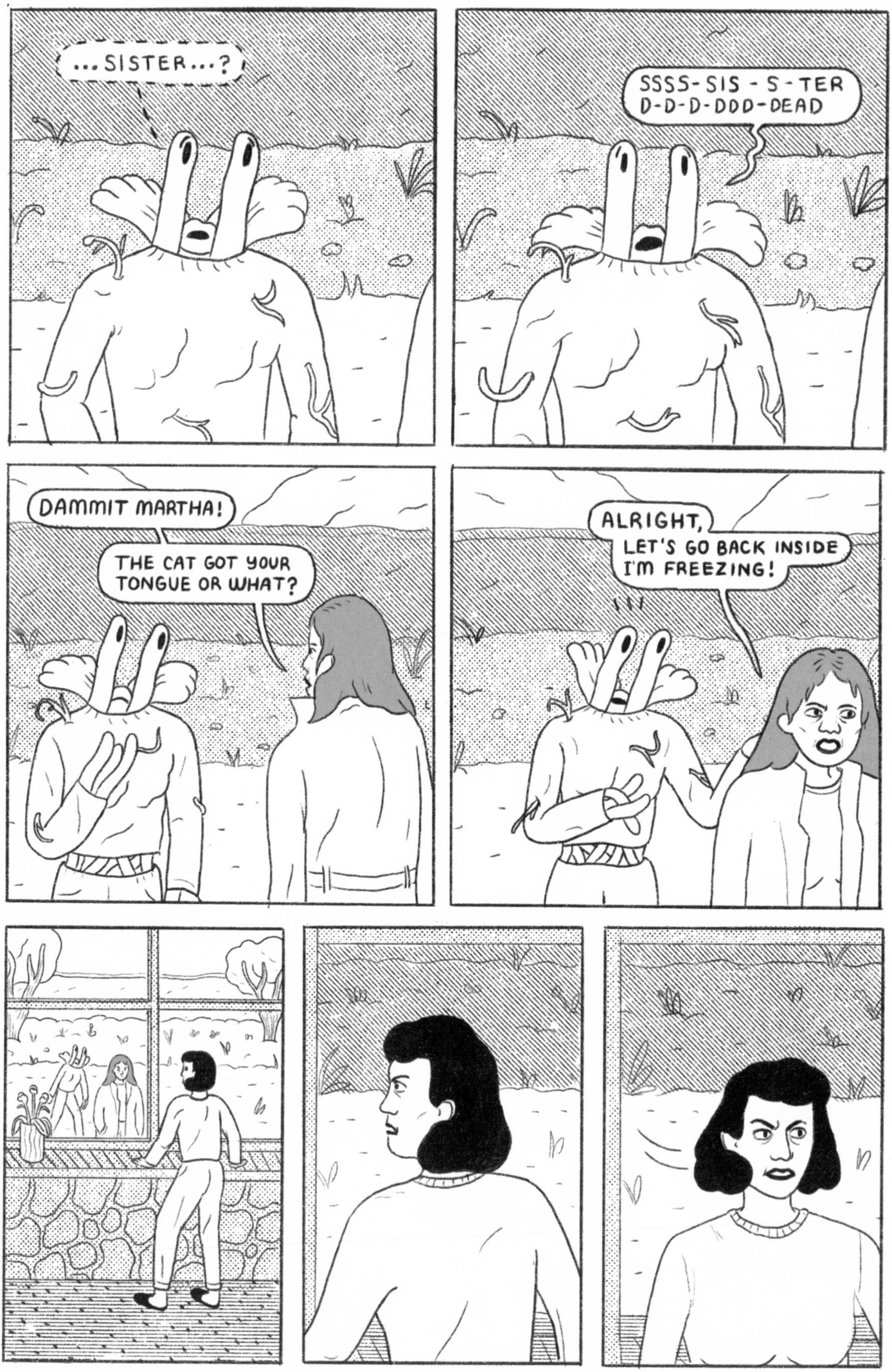
...SISTER...?
SSSS-SIS-S-TER D-D-D-DDD-DEAD
DAMMIT MARTHA!
THE CAT GOT YOUR TONGUE OR WHAT?
ALRIGHT, LET'S GO BACK INSIDE I'M FREEZING!

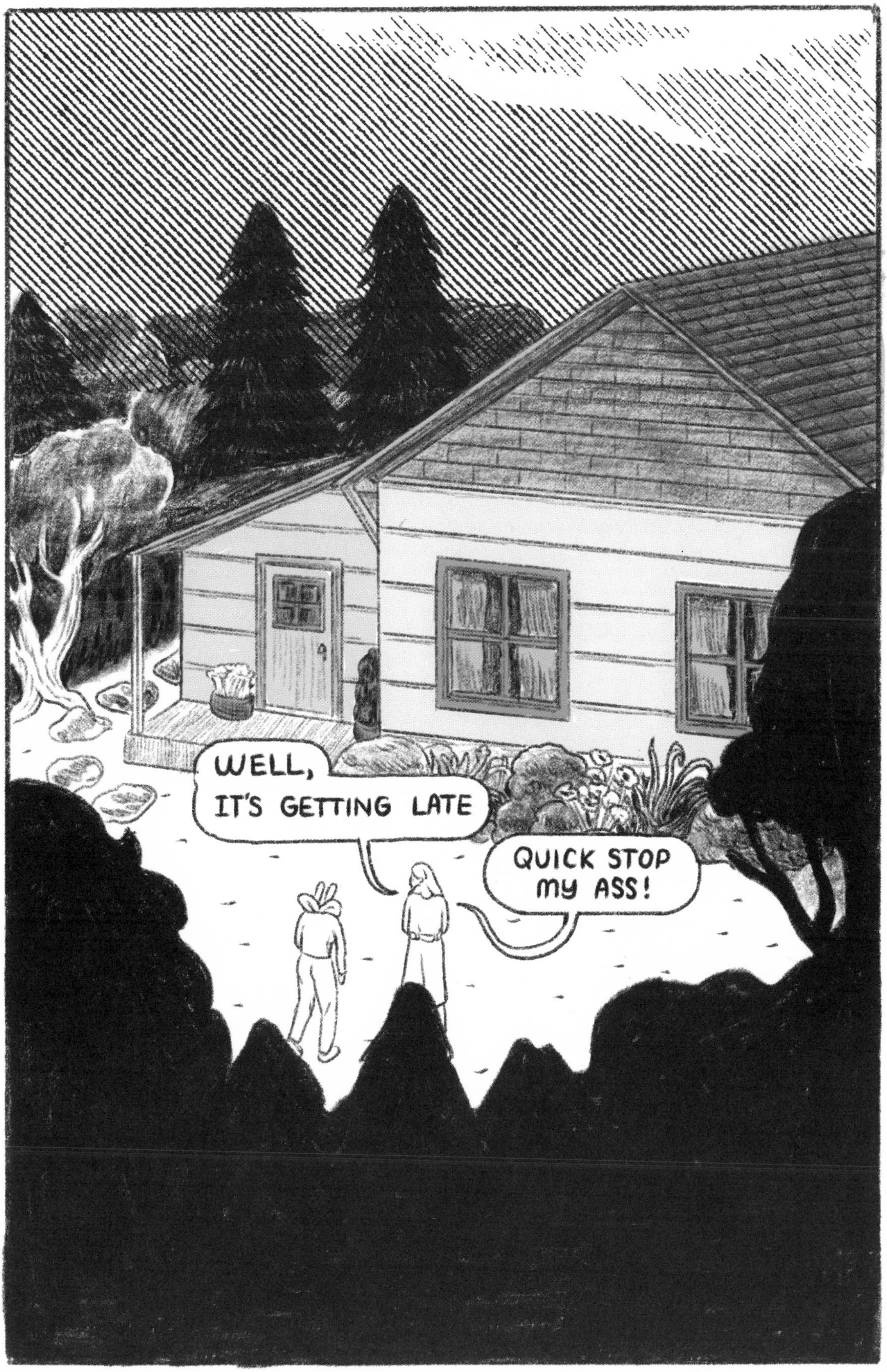
WELL, IT'S GETTING LATE
QUICK STOP MY ASS!

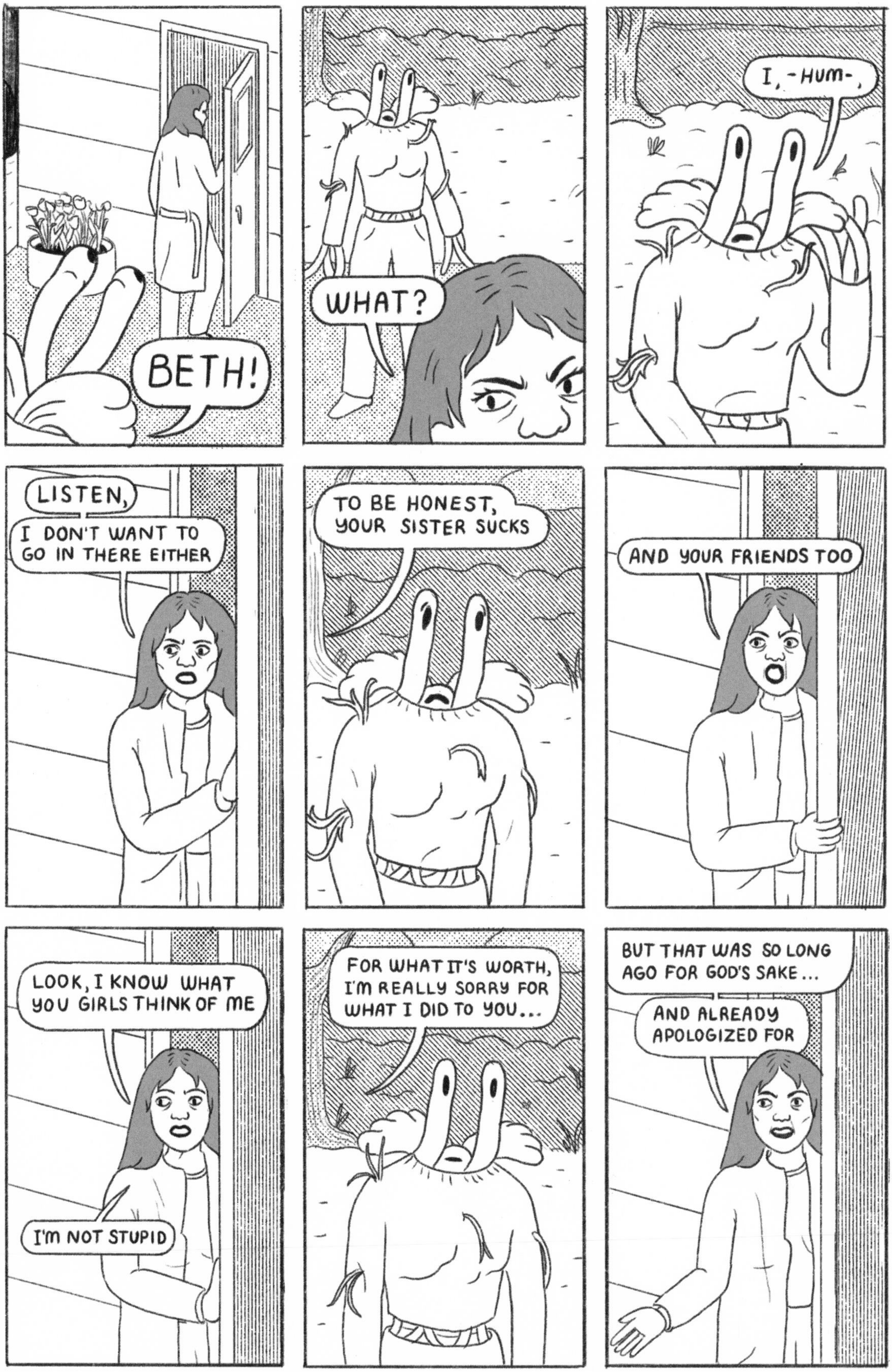
BETH!
WHAT?
I, -HUM-,
LISTEN,
I DON'T WANT TO GO IN THERE EITHER
TO BE HONEST, YOUR SISTER SUCKS
AND YOUR FRIENDS TOO
LOOK, I KNOW WHAT YOU GIRLS THINK OF ME
I'M NOT STUPID
FOR WHAT IT'S WORTH, I'M REALLY SORRY FOR WHAT I DID TO YOU...
BUT THAT WAS SO LONG AGO FOR GOD'S SAKE...
AND ALREADY APOLOGIZED FOR

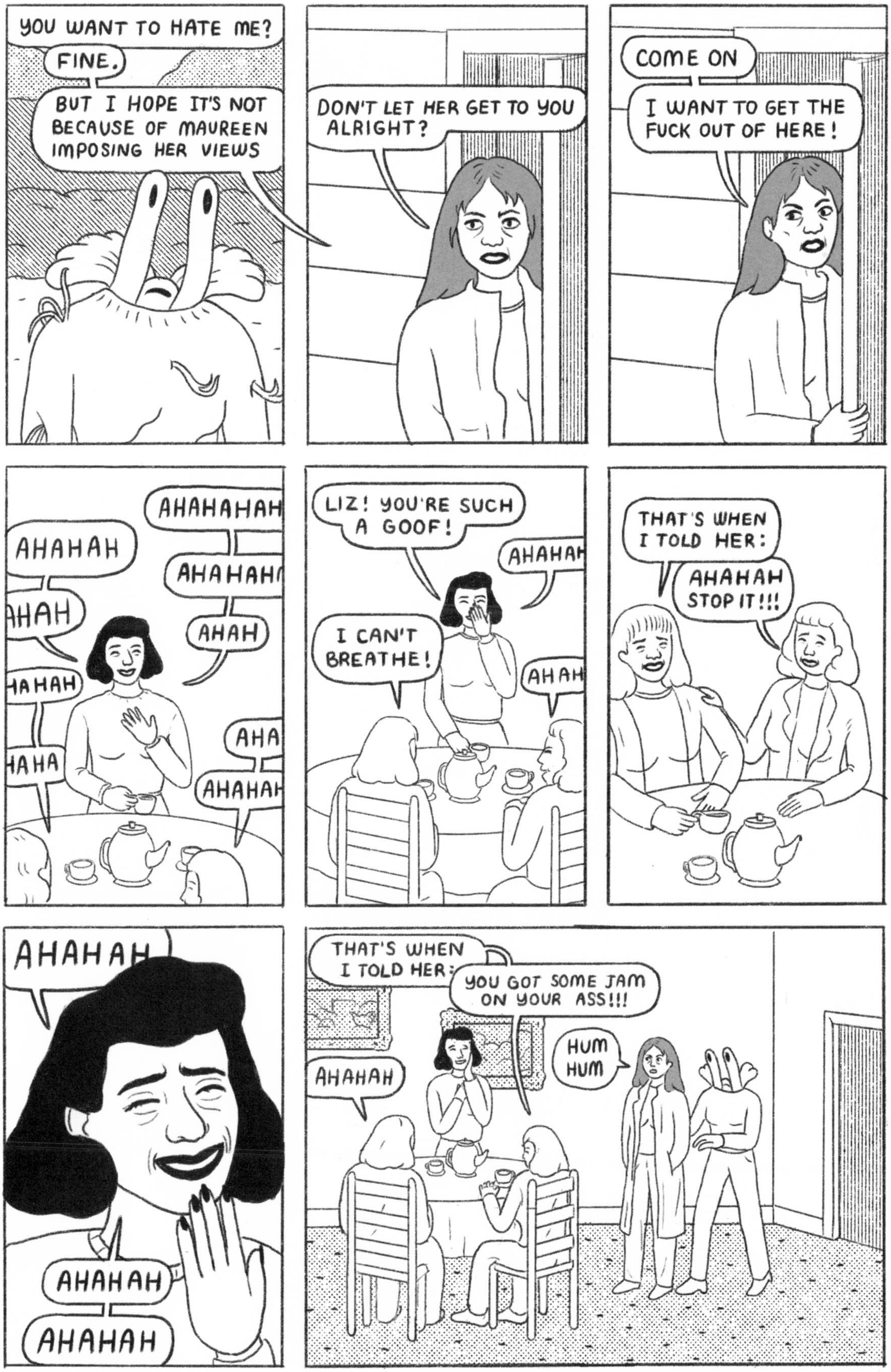
YOU WANT TO HATE ME?
FINE.
BUT I HOPE IT'S NOT BECAUSE OF MAUREEN IMPOSING HER VIEWS
DON'T LET HER GET TO YOU ALRIGHT?
COME ON
I WANT TO GET THE FUCK OUT OF HERE!
AHAHAH
AHAHAHAH
AHAHAH
AHAH
AHAH
HAHAH
AHA
HAHA
AHAHAH
LIZ! YOU'RE SUCH A GOOF!
AHAHAH
I CAN'T BREATHE!
AHAH
THAT'S WHEN I TOLD HER:
AHAHAH STOP IT!!!
AHAHAH
AHAHAH
AHAHAH
THAT'S WHEN I TOLD HER:
YOU GOT SOME JAM ON YOUR ASS!!!
AHAHAH
HUM HUM

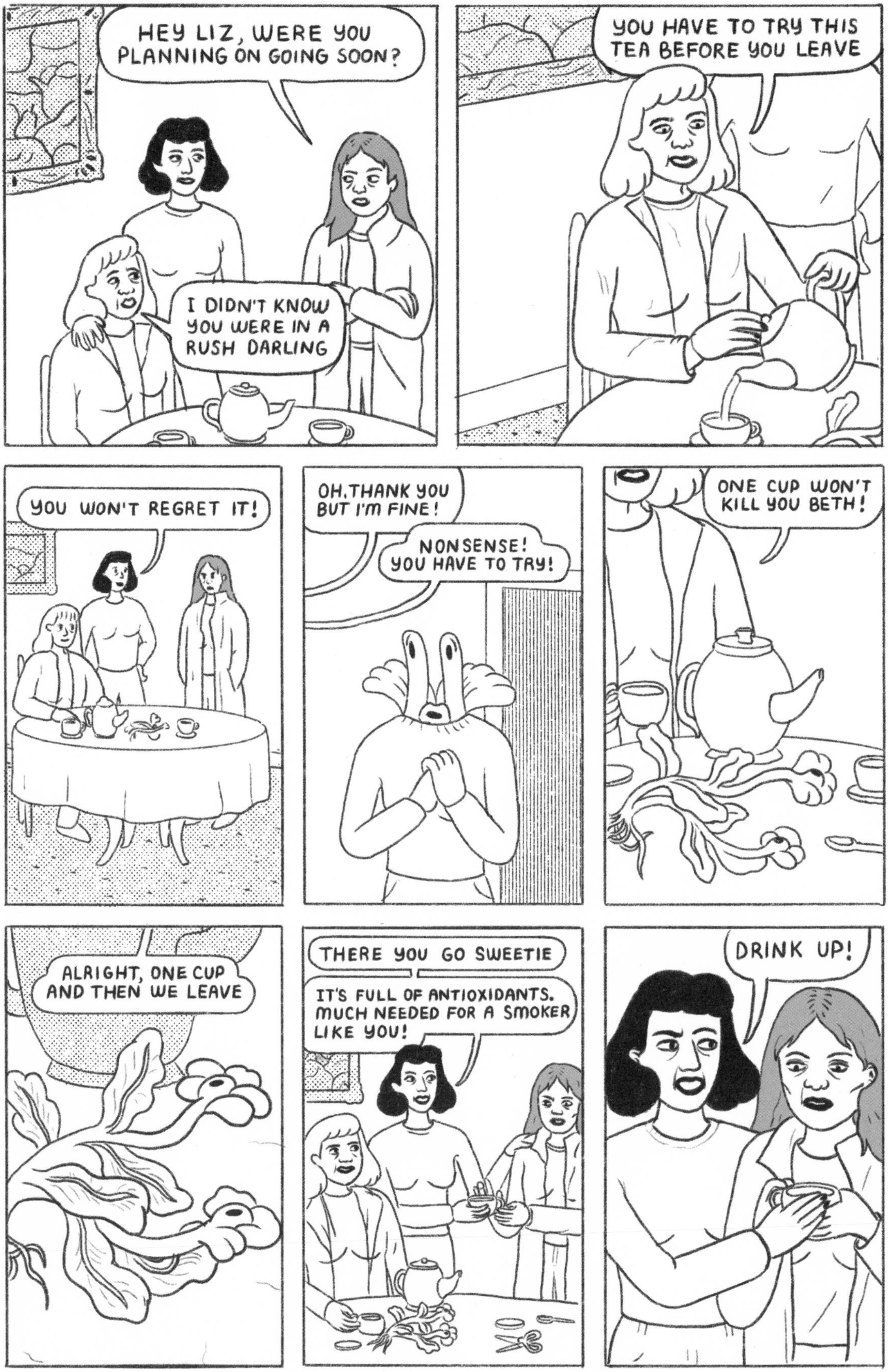
HEY LIZ, WERE YOU PLANNING ON GOING SOON?
I DIDN'T KNOW YOU WERE IN A RUSH DARLING
YOU HAVE TO TRY THIS TEA BEFORE YOU LEAVE
YOU WON'T REGRET IT!
OH, THANK YOU BUT I'M FINE!
NONSENSE! YOU HAVE TO TRY!
ONE CUP WON'T KILL YOU BETH!
ALRIGHT, ONE CUP AND THEN WE LEAVE
THERE YOU GO SWEETIE
IT'S FULL OF ANTIOXIDANTS. MUCH NEEDED FOR A SMOKER LIKE YOU!
DRINK UP!

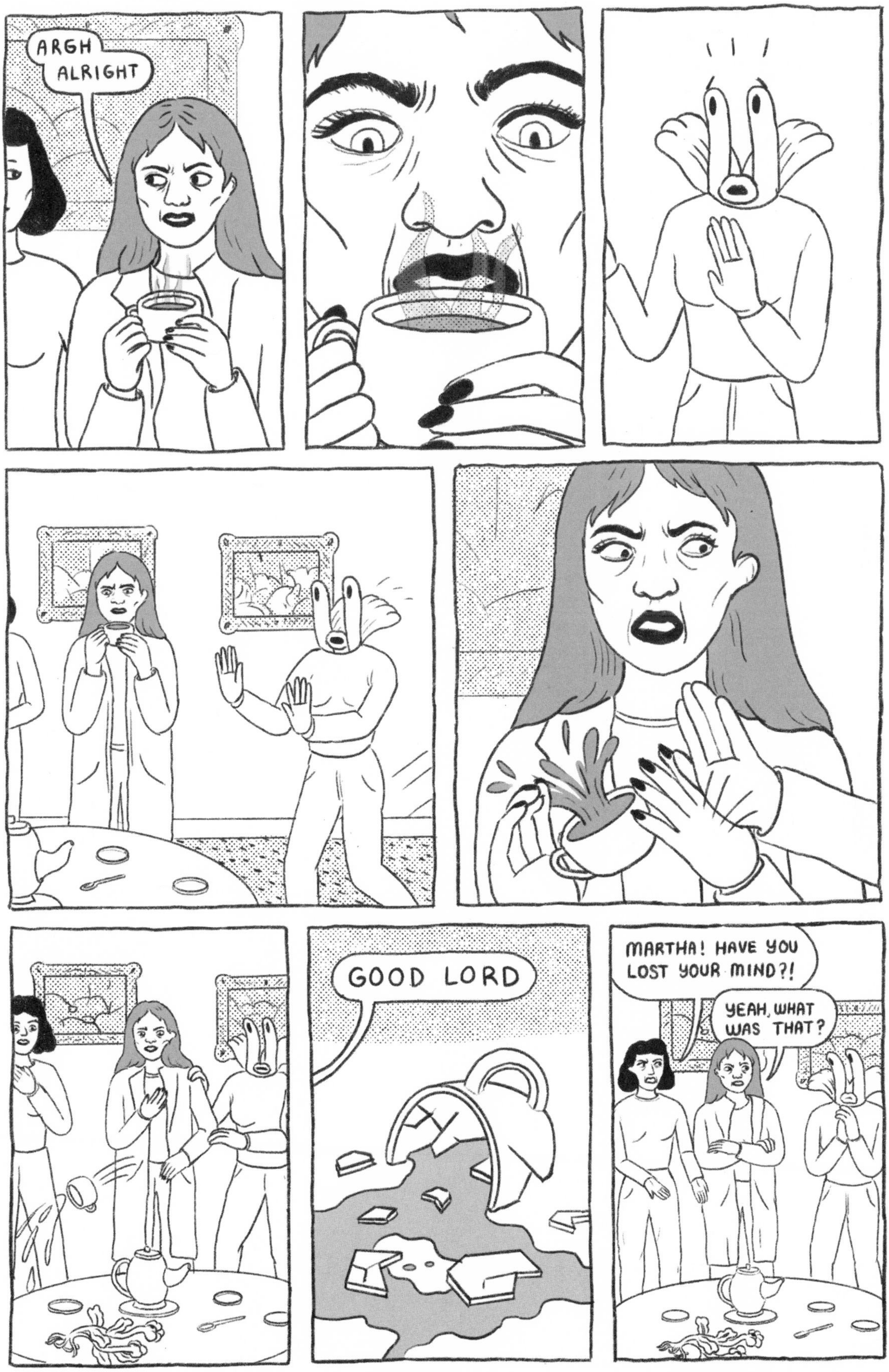
ARGH ALRIGHT
GOOD LORD
MARTHA! HAVE YOU LOST YOUR MIND?!
YEAH, WHAT WAS THAT?

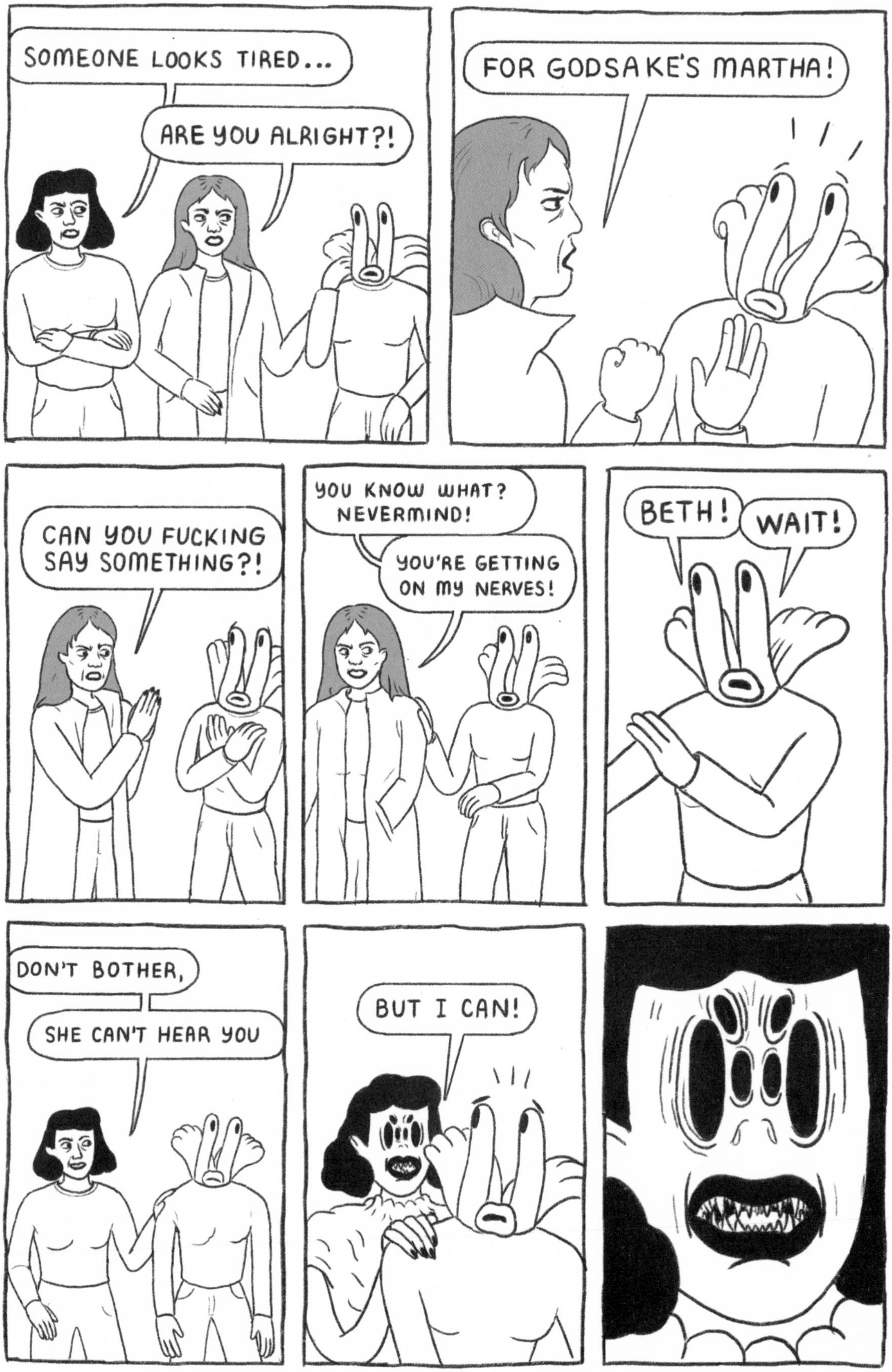
SOMEONE LOOKS TIRED...
ARE YOU ALRIGHT?!
FOR GODSAKE'S MARTHA!
CAN YOU FUCKING SAY SOMETHING?!
YOU KNOW WHAT? NEVERMIND!
YOU'RE GETTING ON MY NERVES!
BETH!
WAIT!
DON'T BOTHER,
SHE CAN'T HEAR YOU
BUT I CAN!

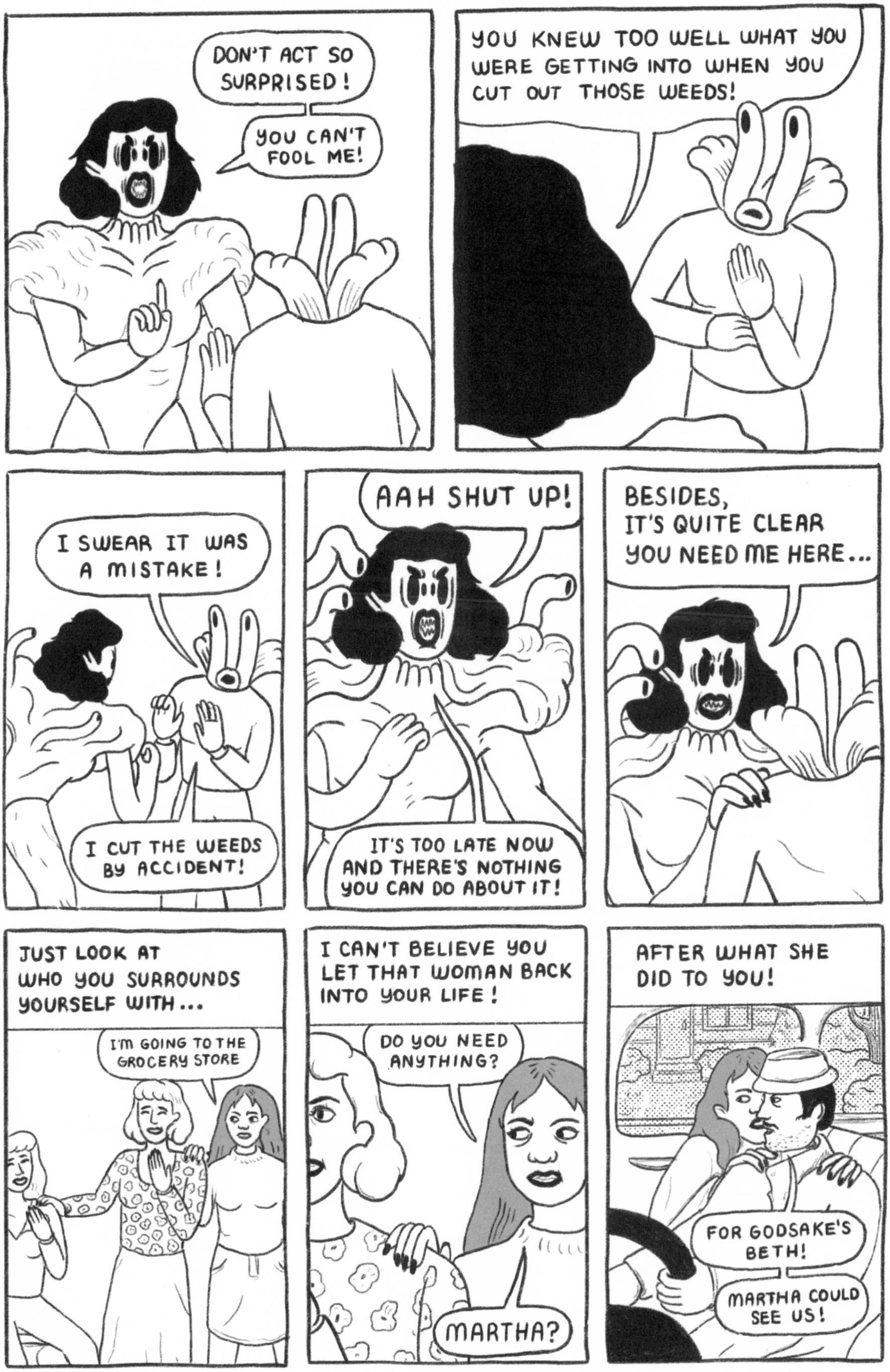
DON'T ACT SO SURPRISED!
YOU CAN'T FOOL ME!
YOU KNEW TOO WELL WHAT YOU WERE GETTING INTO WHEN YOU CUT OUT THOSE WEEDS!
I SWEAR IT WAS A MISTAKE!
I CUT THE WEEDS BY ACCIDENT!
AAH SHUT UP!
IT'S TOO LATE NOW AND THERE'S NOTHING YOU CAN DO ABOUT IT!
BESIDES, IT'S QUITE CLEAR YOU NEED ME HERE...
JUST LOOK AT WHO YOU SURROUNDS YOURSELF WITH...
I'M GOING TO THE GROCERY STORE
I CAN'T BELIEVE YOU LET THAT WOMAN BACK INTO YOUR LIFE!
DO YOU NEED ANYTHING?
MARTHA?
AFTER WHAT SHE DID TO YOU!
FOR GODSAKE'S BETH!
MARTHA COULD SEE US!

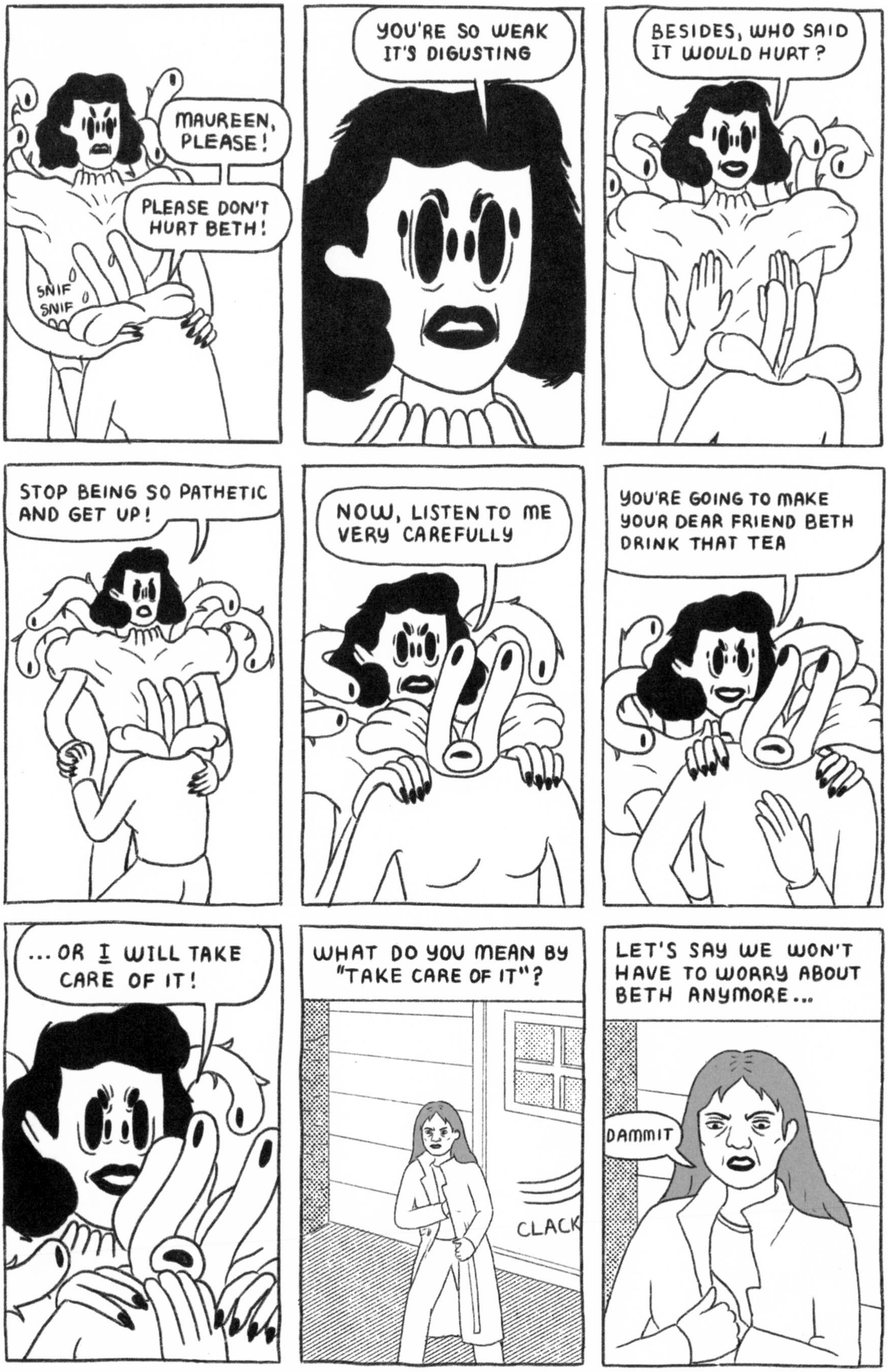
MAUREEN, PLEASE!
PLEASE DON'T HURT BETH!
SNIF SNIF
YOU'RE SO WEAK IT'S DIGUSTING
BESIDES, WHO SAID IT WOULD HURT?
STOP BEING SO PATHETIC AND GET UP!
NOW, LISTEN TO ME VERY CAREFULLY
YOU'RE GOING TO MAKE YOUR DEAR FRIEND BETH DRINK THAT TEA
... OR I WILL TAKE CARE OF IT!
WHAT DO YOU MEAN BY "TAKE CARE OF IT"?
CLACK
LET'S SAY WE WON'T HAVE TO WORRY ABOUT BETH ANYMORE...
DAMMIT

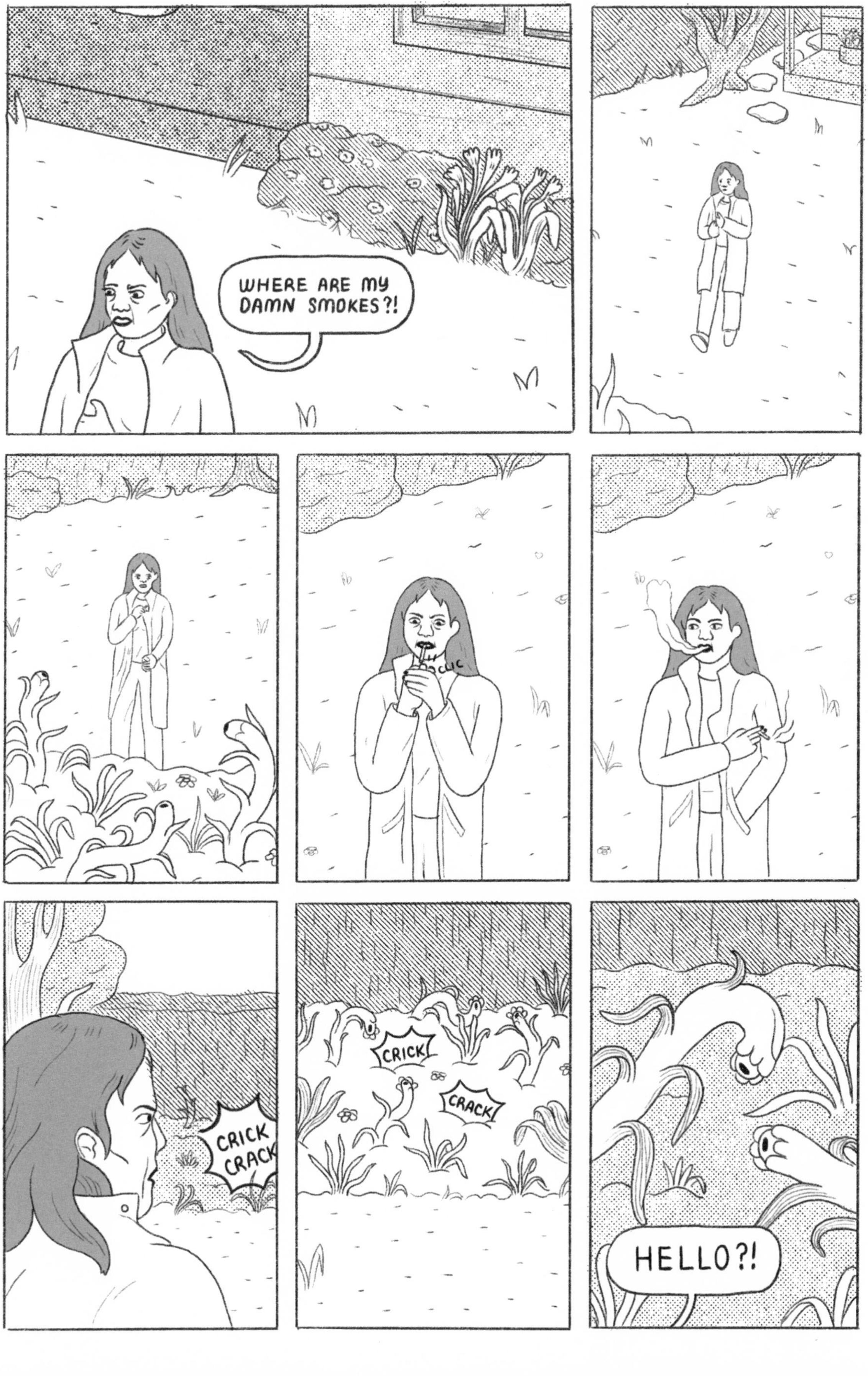
WHERE ARE MY DAMN SMOKES?!
CLIC
CRICK CRACK
CRICK
CRACK
HELLO?!

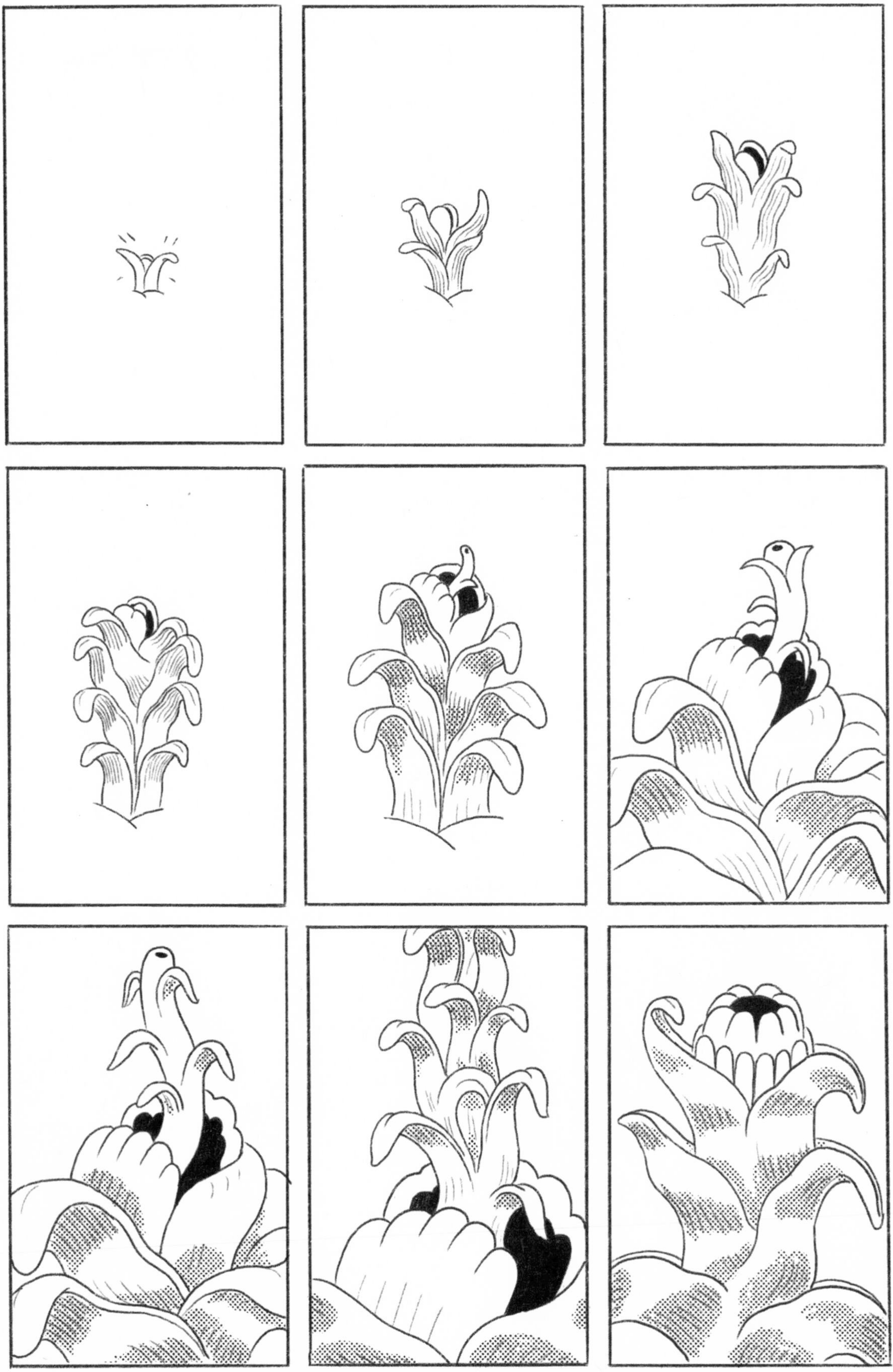

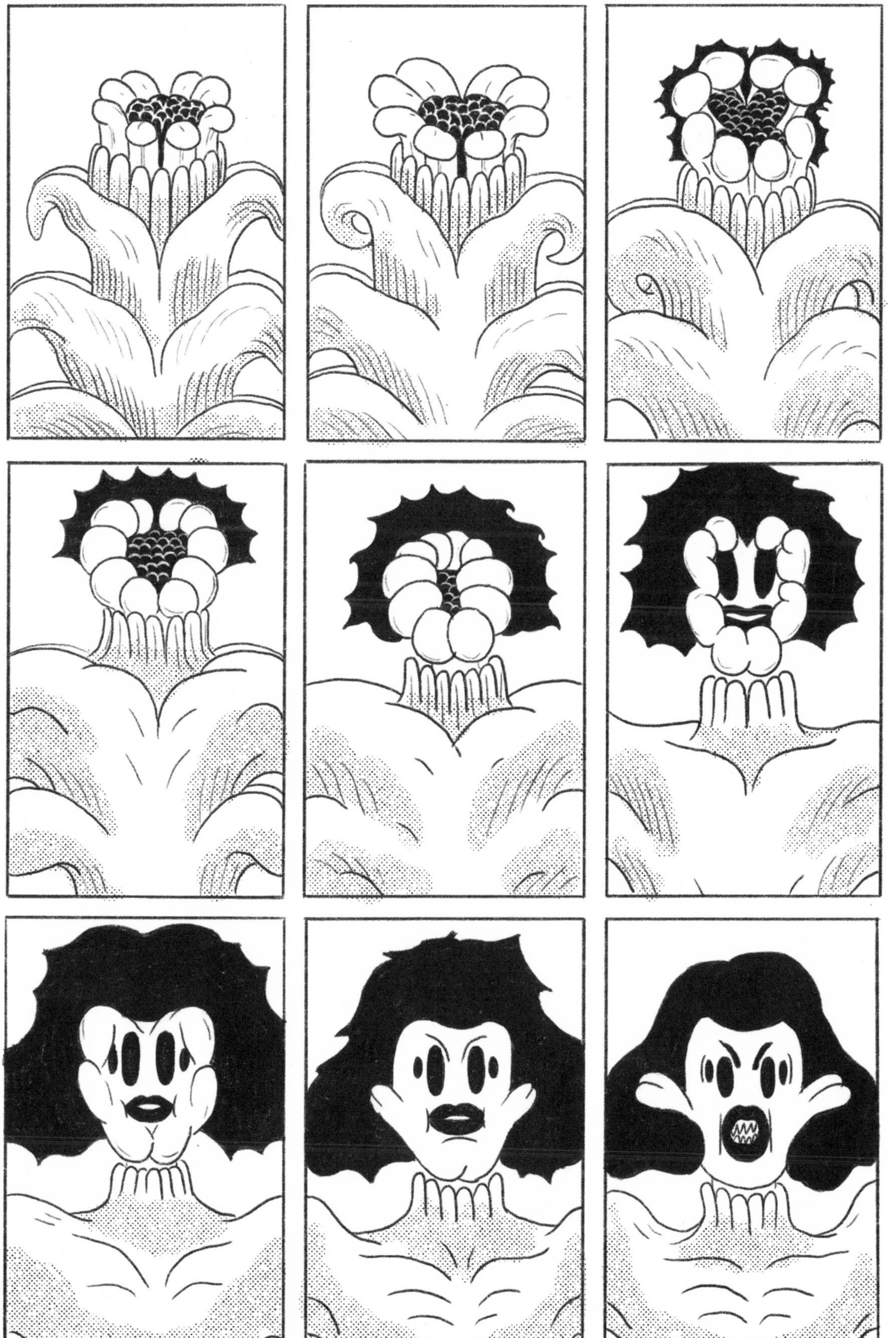

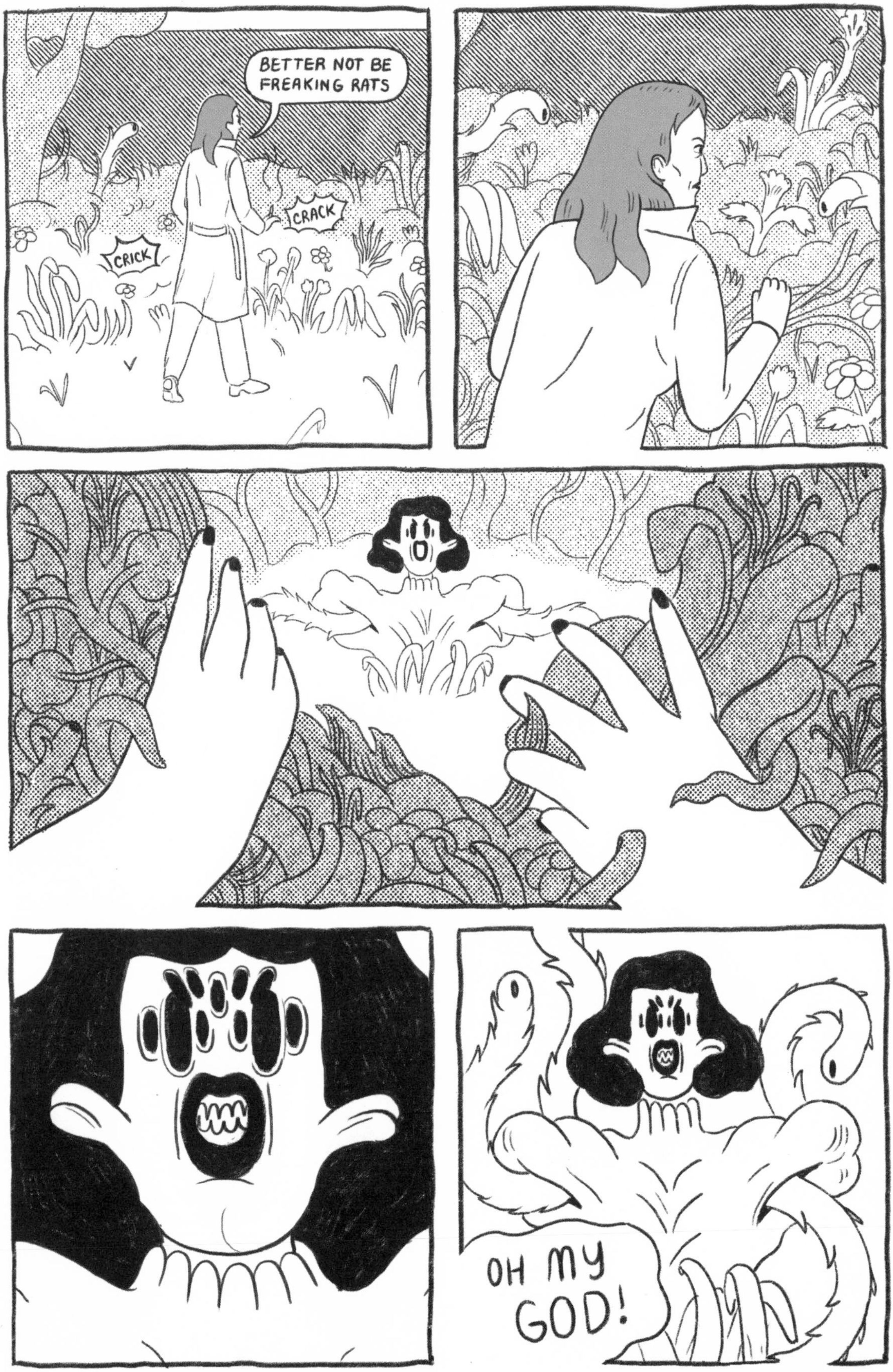

BETTER NOT BE FREAKING RATS
CRICK
CRACK
OH MY GOD!

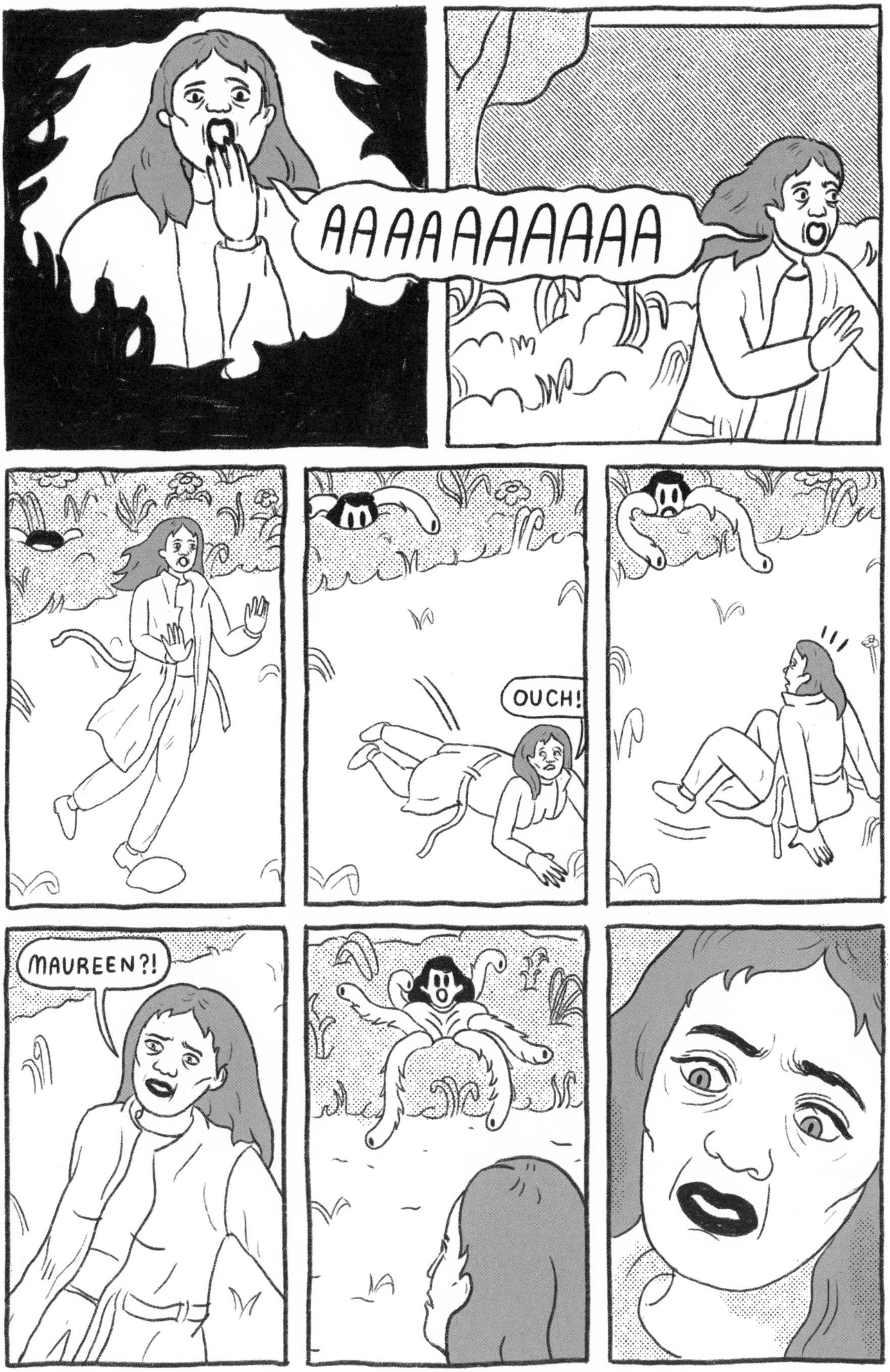
AAAAAAAAAA
OUCH!
MAUREEN?!

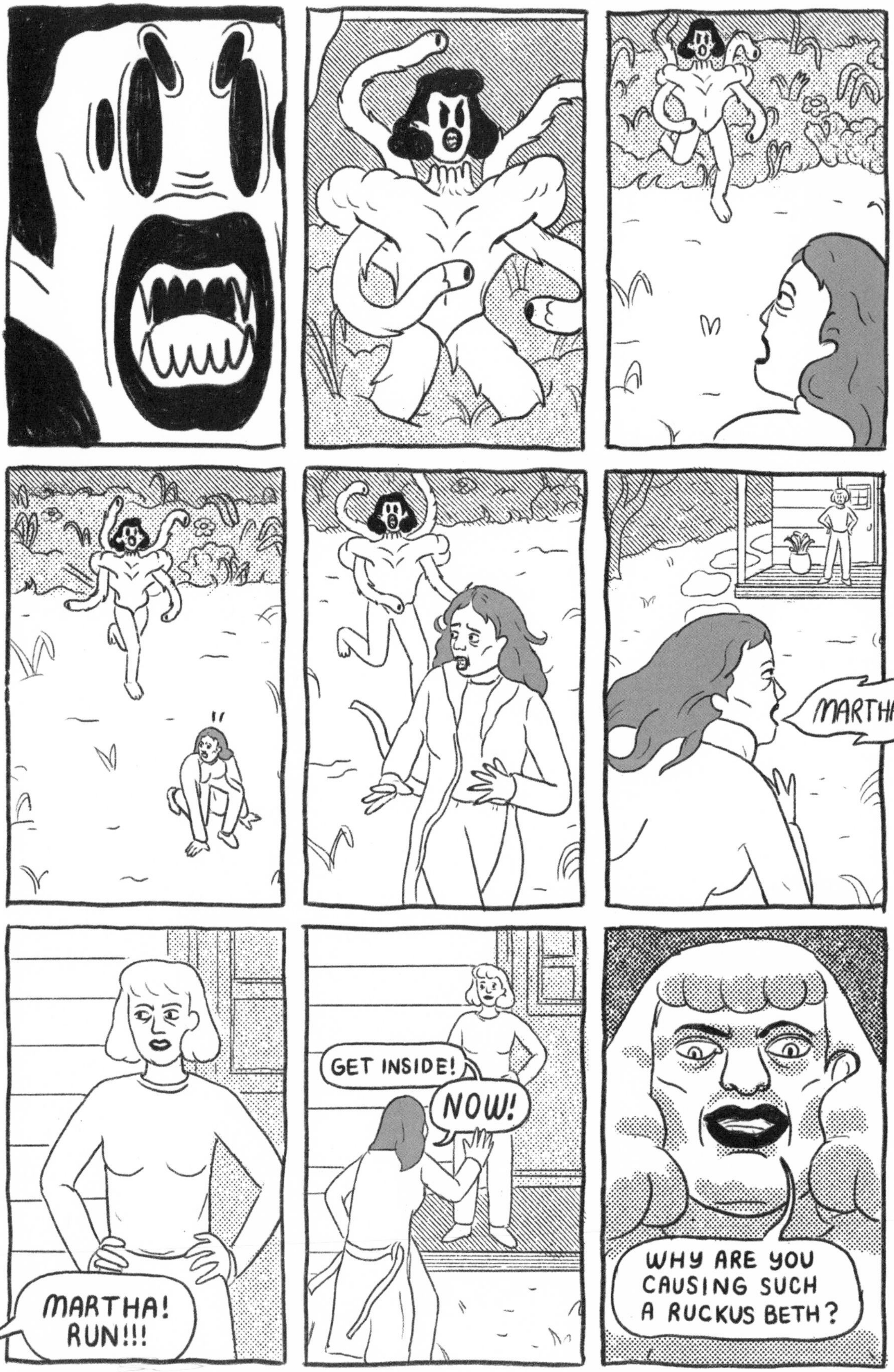
MARTHA!
MARTHA! RUN!!!
GET INSIDE!
NOW!
WHY ARE YOU CAUSING SUCH A RUCKUS BETH?

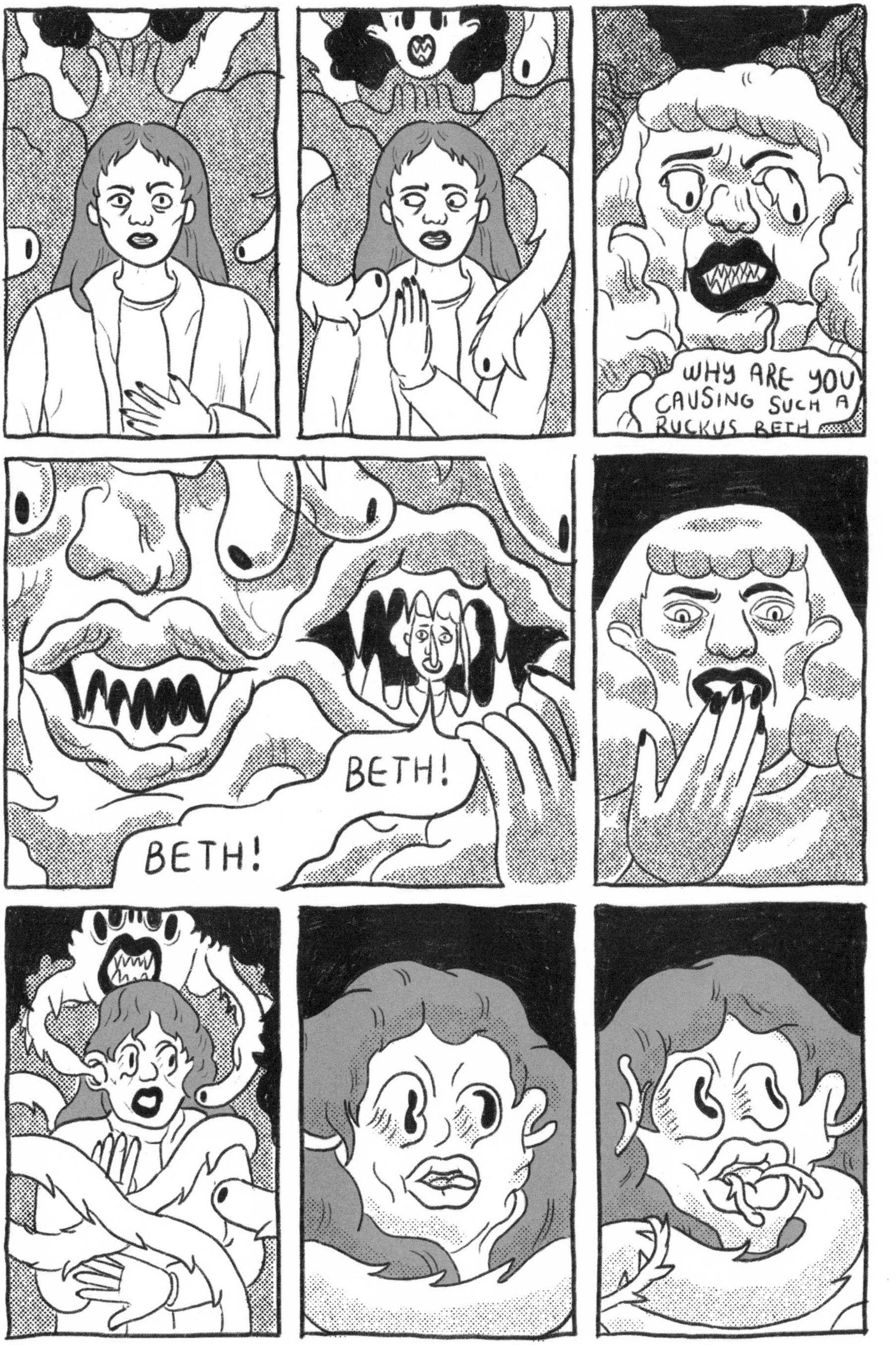
WHY ARE YOU CAUSING SUCH A RUCKUS BETH
BETH!
BETH!

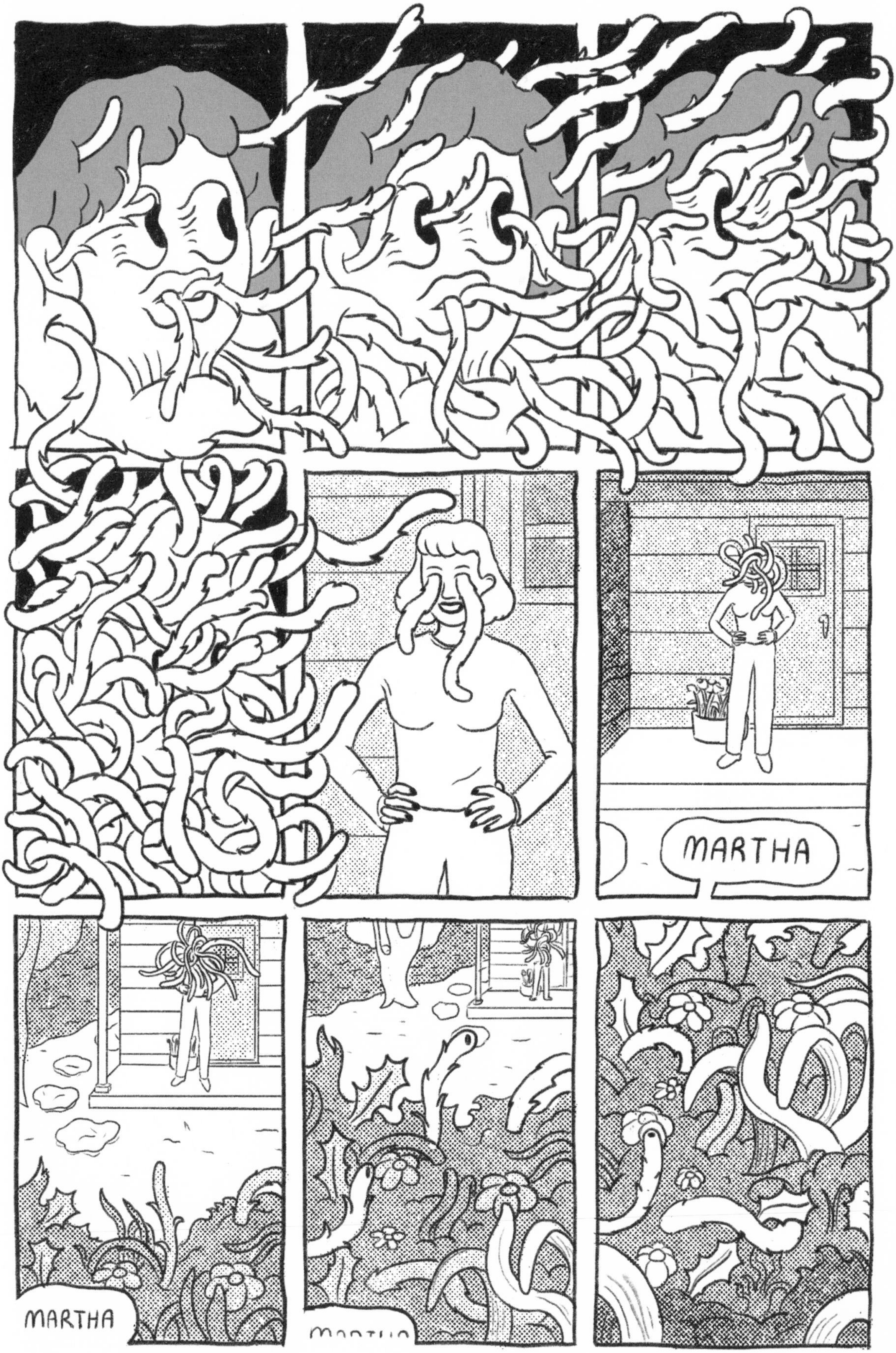
MARTHA
MARTHA

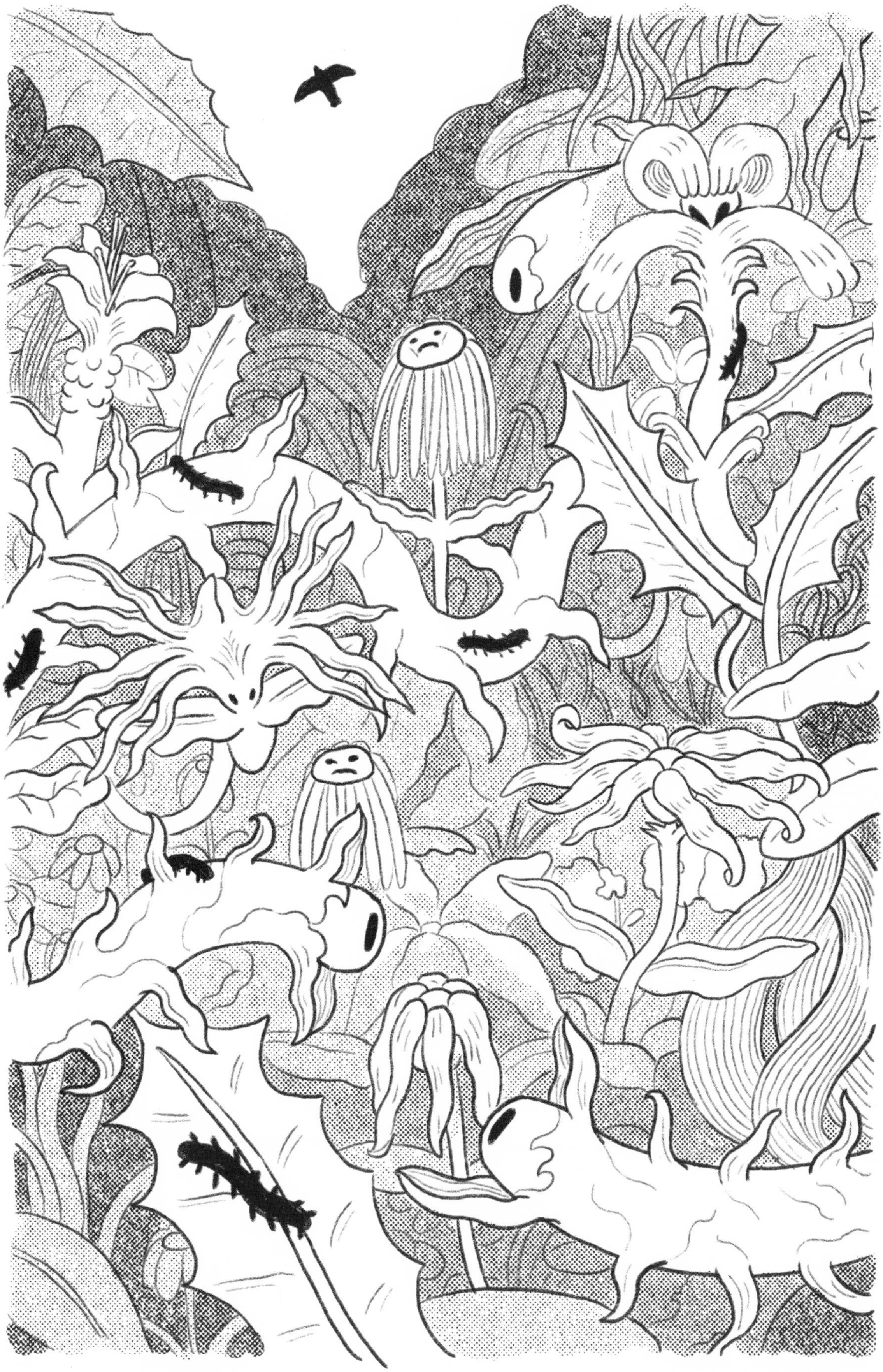

THE FOLLOWING SPRING

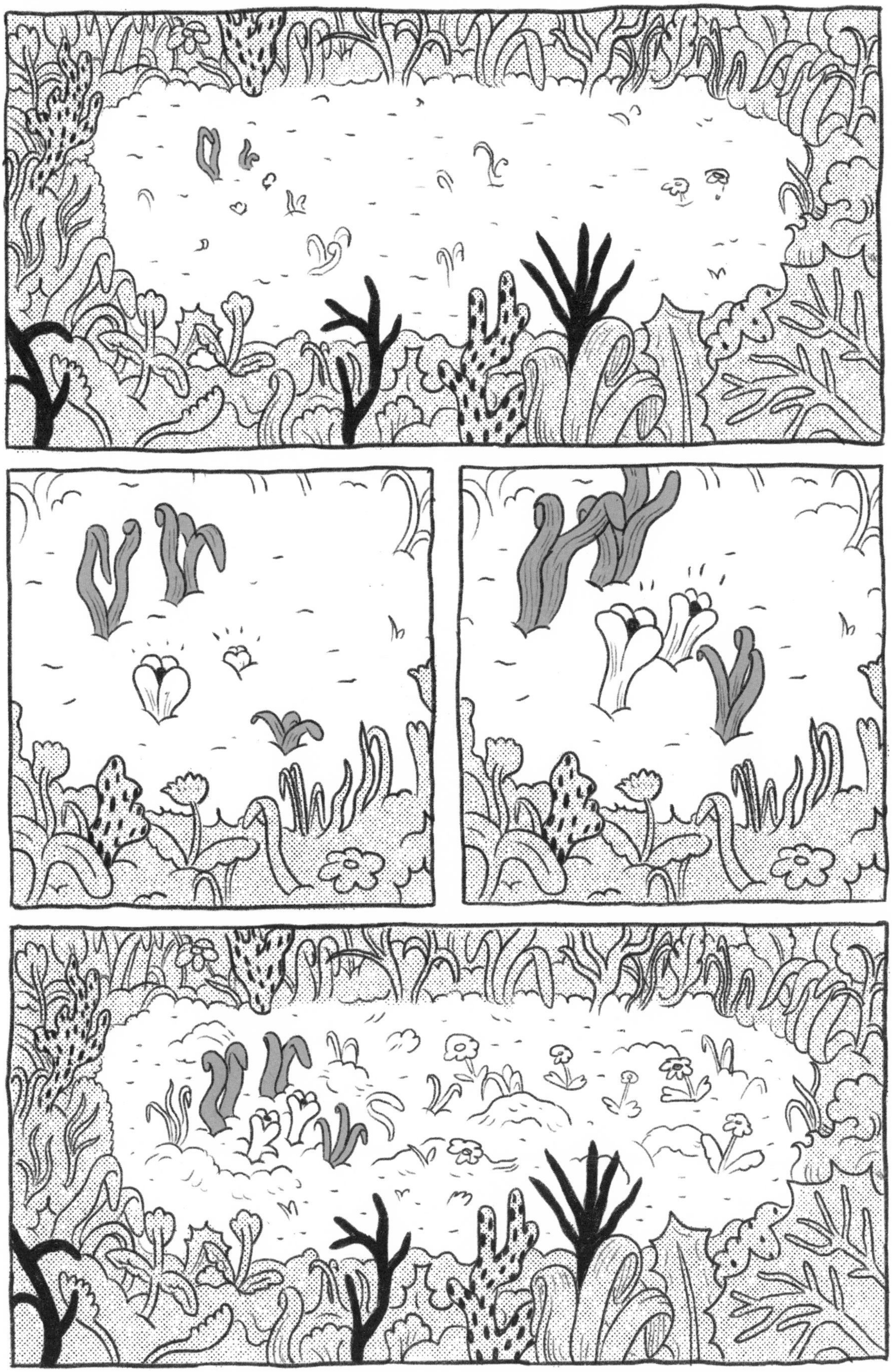

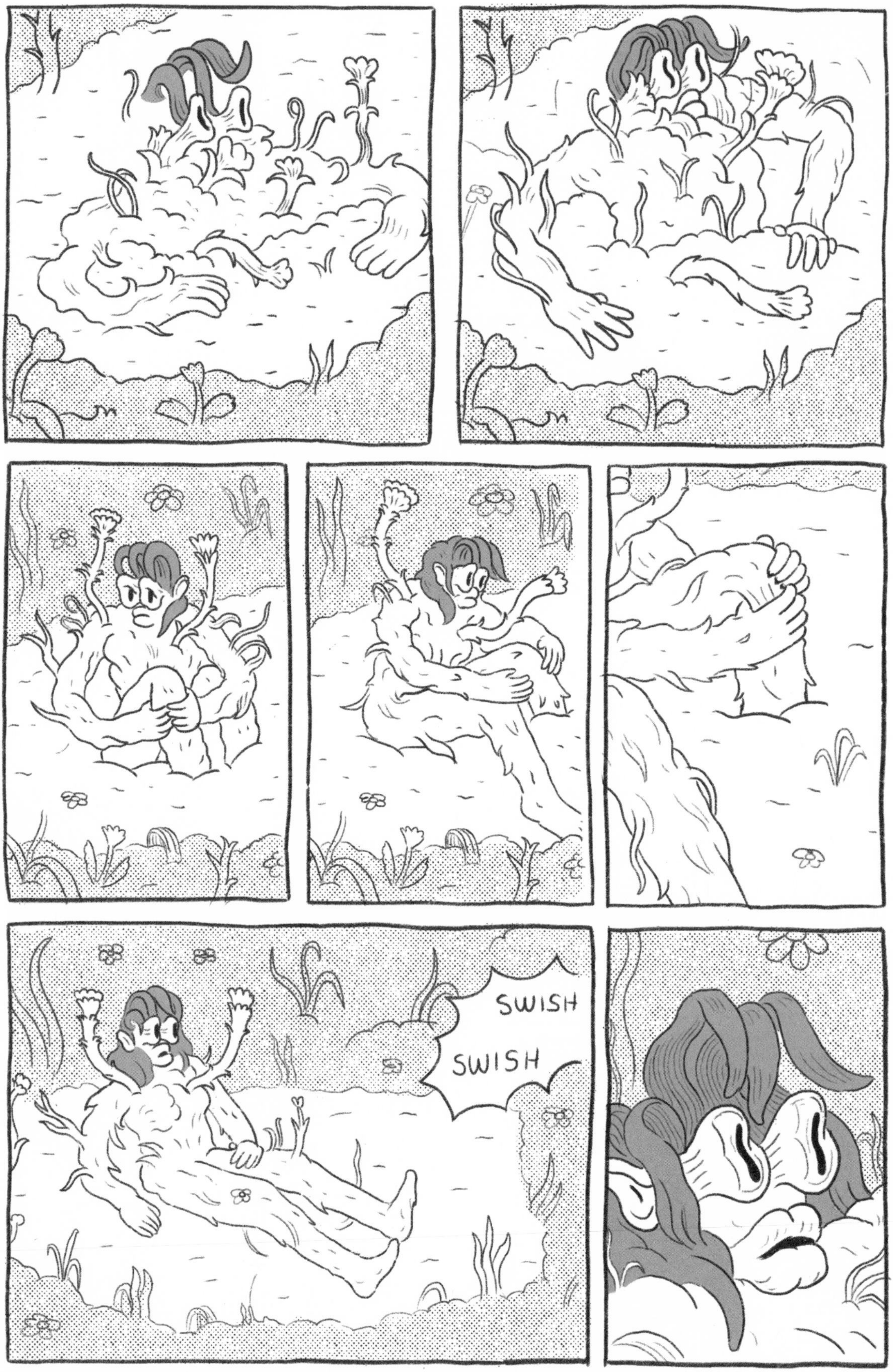
SWISH
SWISH

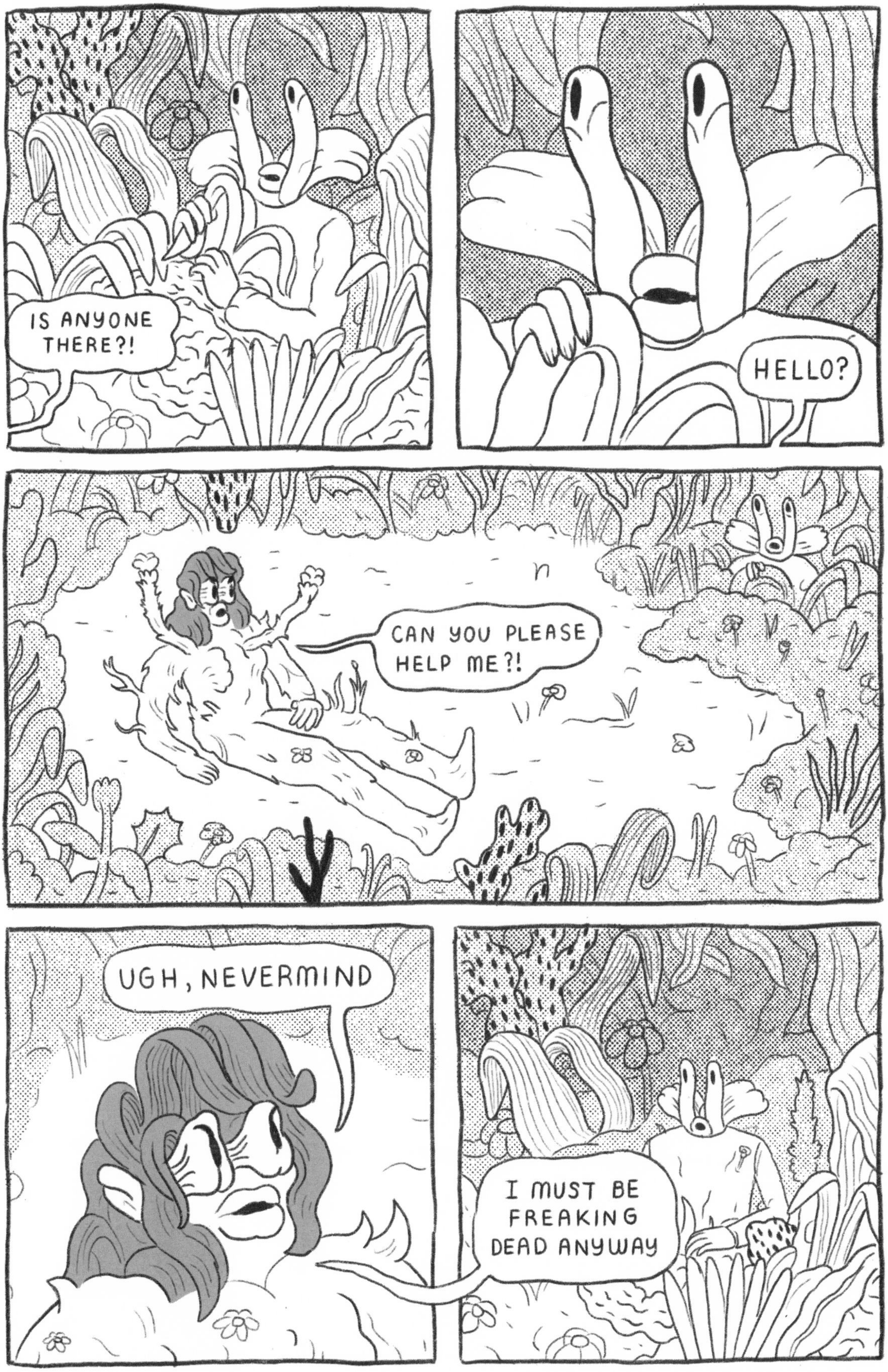
IS ANYONE THERE?!
HELLO?
CAN YOU PLEASE HELP ME?!
UGH, NEVERMIND
I MUST BE FREAKING DEAD ANYWAY

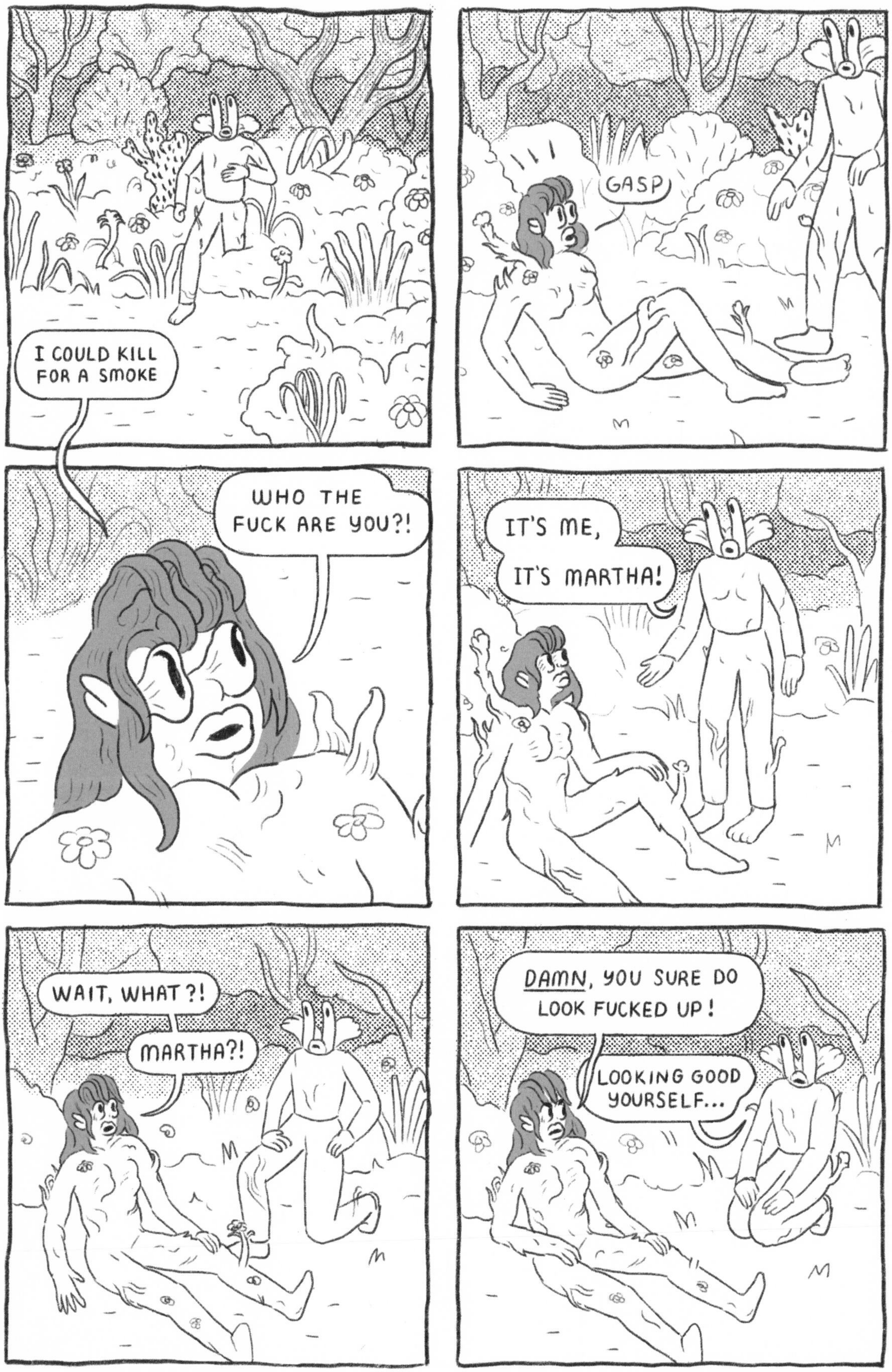
I COULD KILL FOR A SMOKE
GASP
WHO THE FUCK ARE YOU?!
IT'S ME,
IT'S MARTHA!
WAIT, WHAT?!
MARTHA?!
DAMN, YOU SURE DO LOOK FUCKED UP!
LOOKING GOOD YOURSELF...

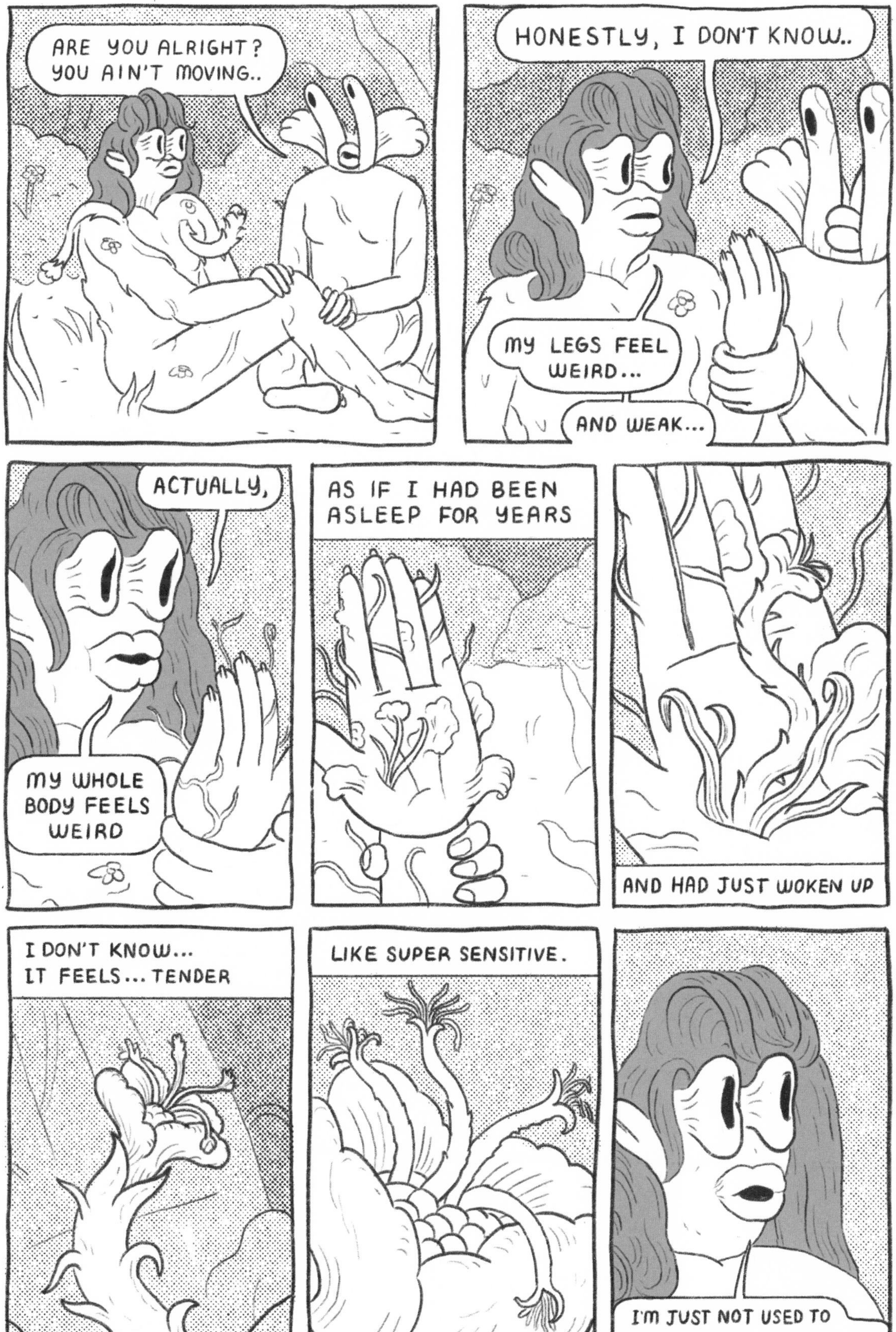
ARE YOU ALRIGHT? YOU AIN'T MOVING..
HONESTLY, I DON'T KNOW..
MY LEGS FEEL WEIRD...
AND WEAK...
ACTUALLY,
MY WHOLE BODY FEELS WEIRD
AS IF I HAD BEEN ASLEEP FOR YEARS
AND HAD JUST WOKEN UP
I DON'T KNOW... IT FEELS... TENDER
LIKE SUPER SENSITIVE.
I'M JUST NOT USED TO FEELING THIS MUCH I GUESS

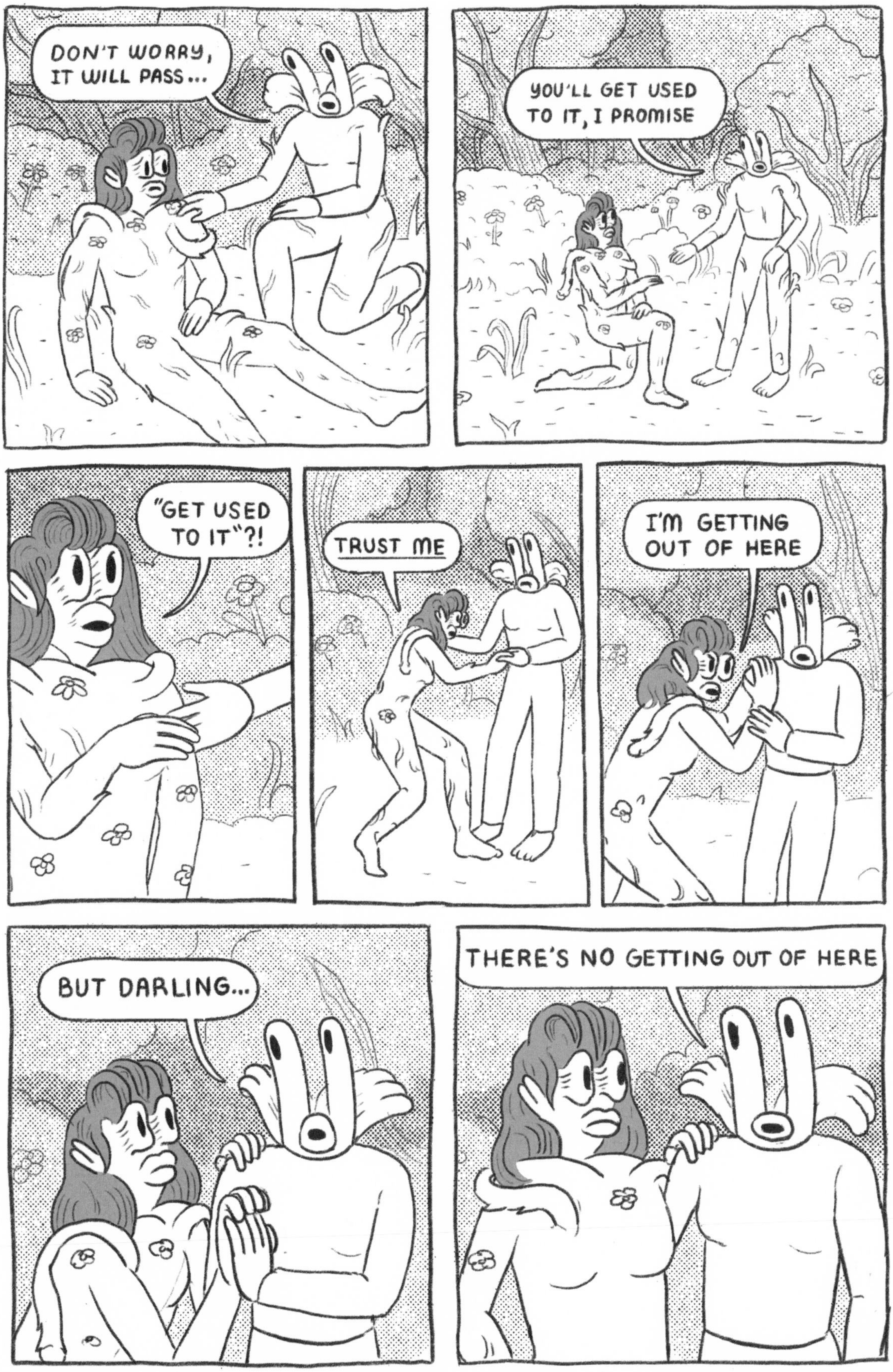
DON'T WORRY, IT WILL PASS...
YOU'LL GET USED TO IT, I PROMISE
"GET USED TO IT"?!
TRUST ME
I'M GETTING OUT OF HERE
BUT DARLING...
THERE'S NO GETTING OUT OF HERE

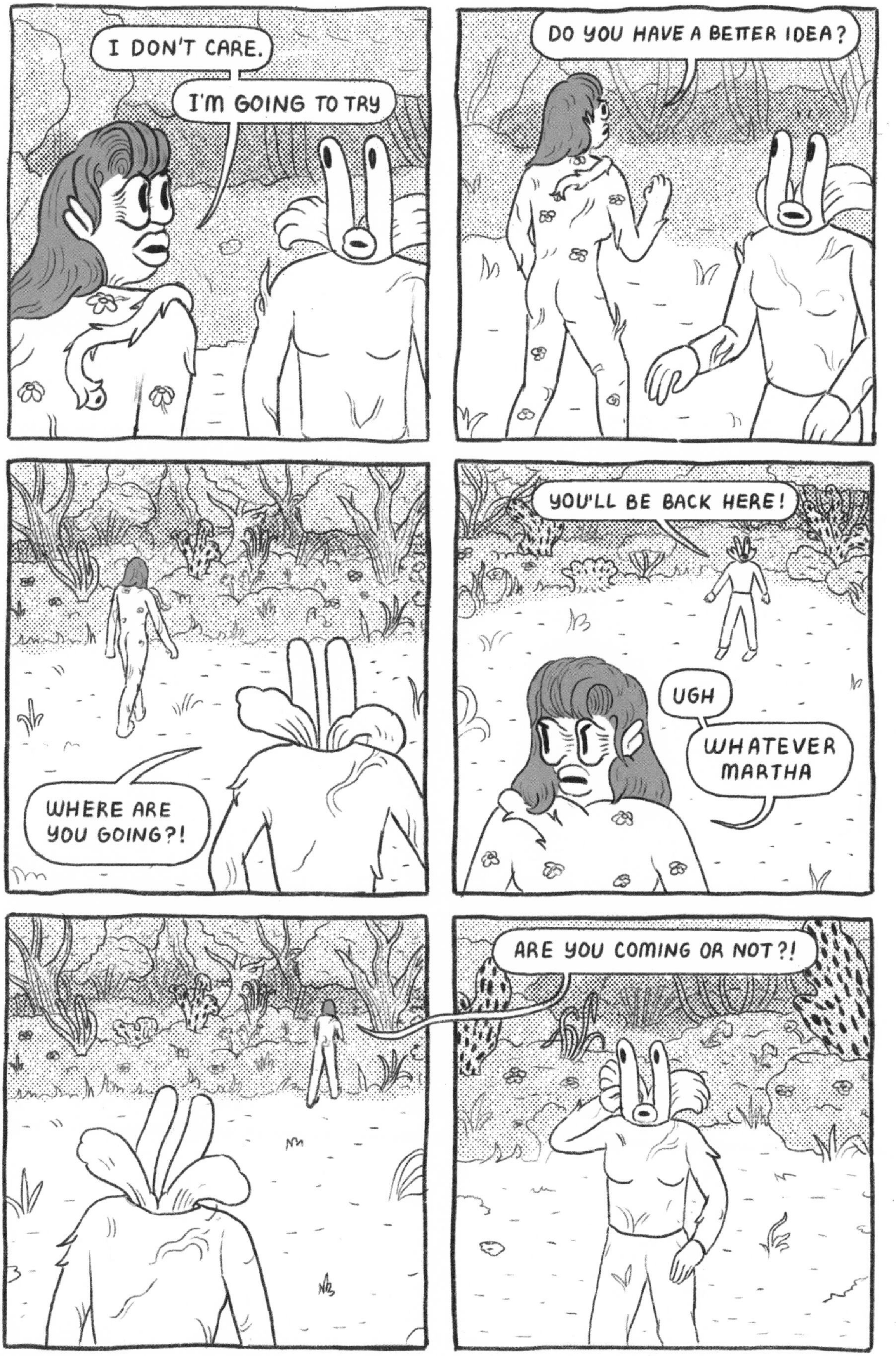
I DON'T CARE.
I'M GOING TO TRY
DO YOU HAVE A BETTER IDEA?
WHERE ARE YOU GOING?!
YOU'LL BE BACK HERE!
UGH
WHATEVER MARTHA
ARE YOU COMING OR NOT?!

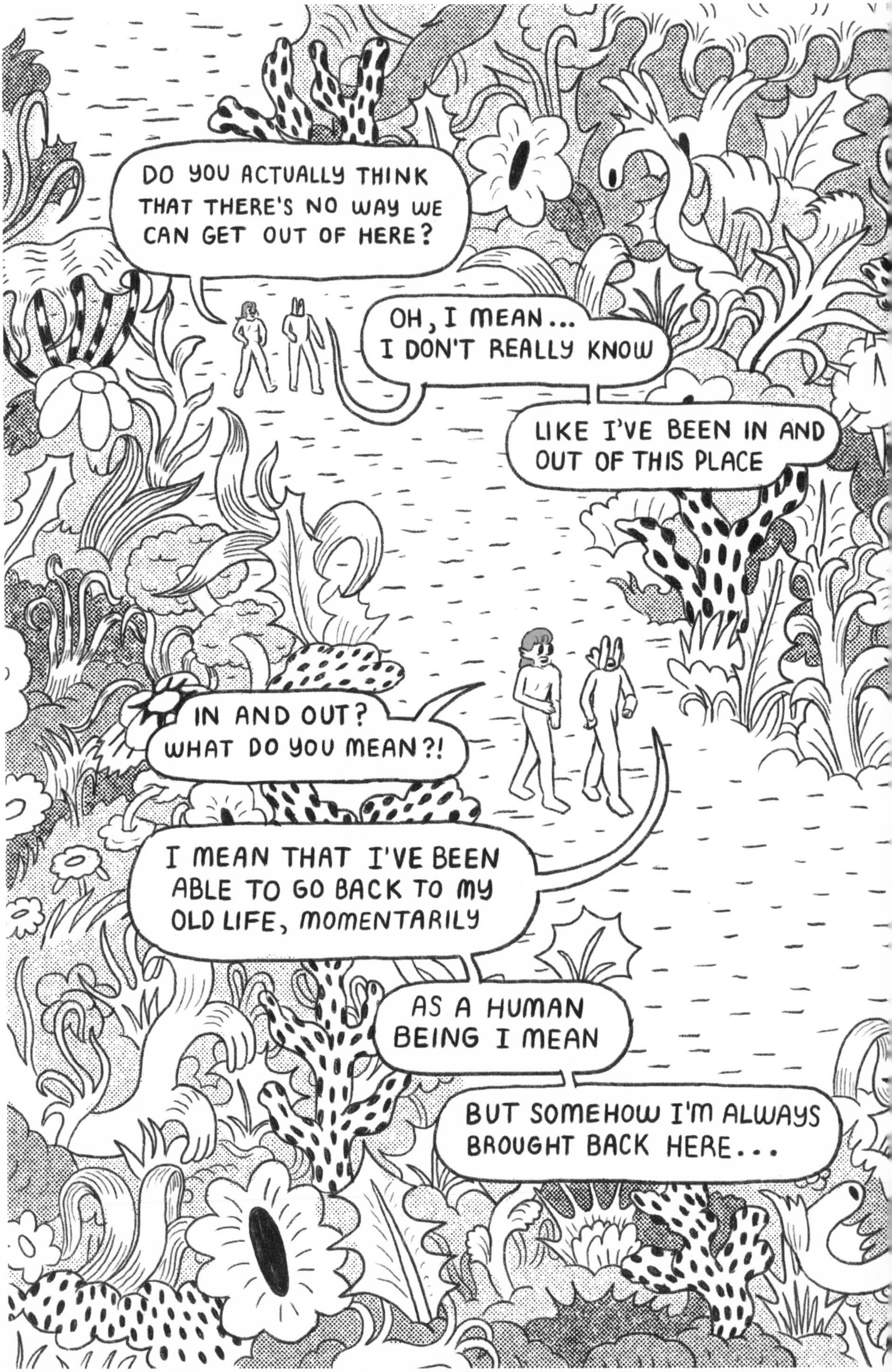
DO YOU ACTUALLY THINK THAT THERE'S NO WAY WE CAN GET OUT OF HERE?
OH, I MEAN... I DON'T REALLY KNOW
LIKE I'VE BEEN IN AND OUT OF THIS PLACE
IN AND OUT? WHAT DO YOU MEAN?!
I MEAN THAT I'VE BEEN ABLE TO GO BACK TO MY OLD LIFE, MOMENTARILY
AS A HUMAN BEING I MEAN
BUT SOMEHOW I'M ALWAYS BROUGHT BACK HERE...

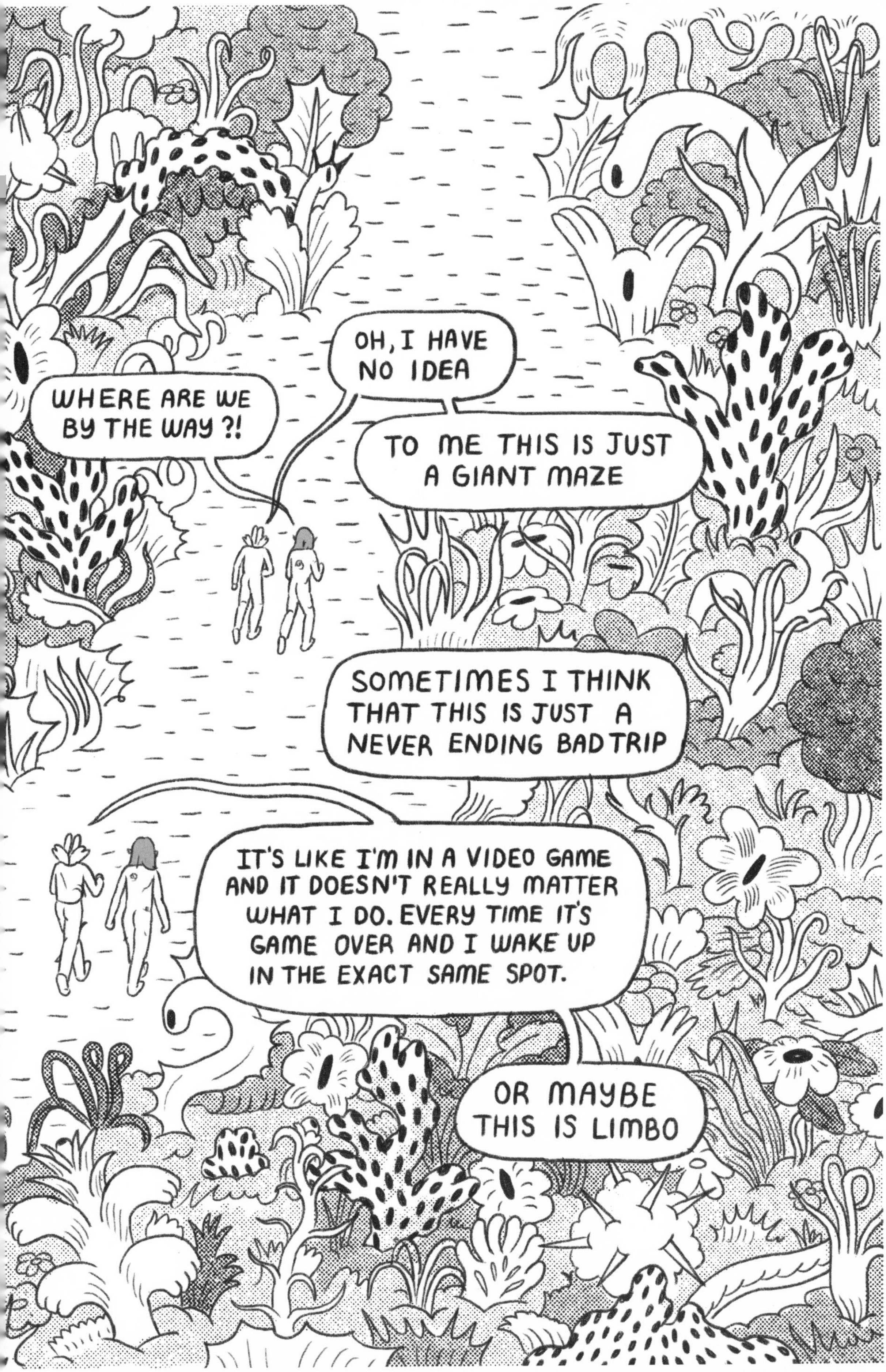
WHERE ARE WE BY THE WAY ?!
OH, I HAVE NO IDEA
TO ME THIS IS JUST A GIANT MAZE
SOMETIMES I THINK THAT THIS IS JUST A NEVER ENDING BAD TRIP
IT'S LIKE I'M IN A VIDEO GAME AND IT DOESN'T REALLY MATTER WHAT I DO. EVERY TIME IT'S GAME OVER AND I WAKE UP IN THE EXACT SAME SPOT.
OR MAYBE THIS IS LIMBO

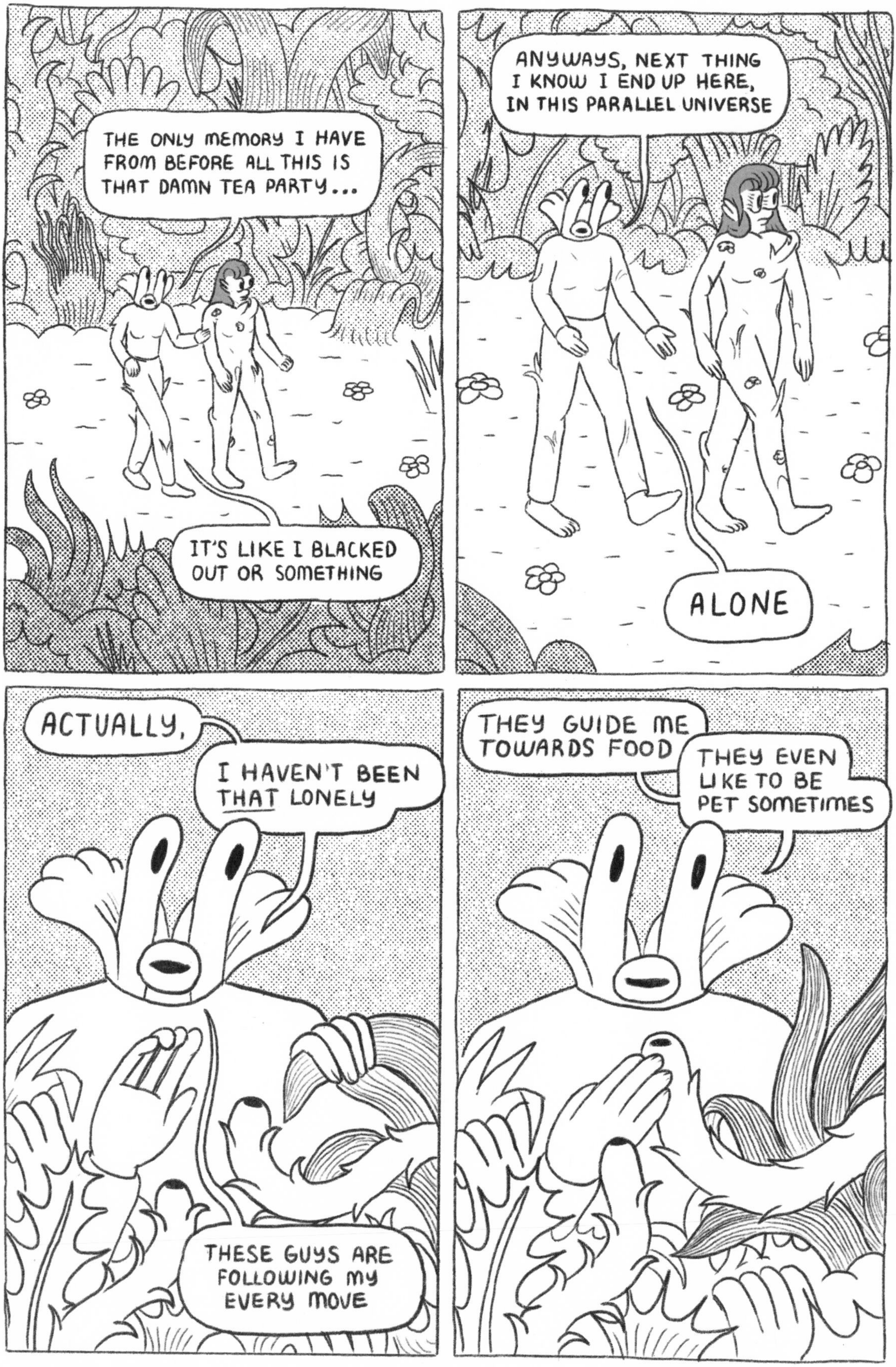
THE ONLY MEMORY I HAVE FROM BEFORE ALL THIS IS THAT DAMN TEA PARTY...
IT'S LIKE I BLACKED OUT OR SOMETHING
ANYWAYS, NEXT THING I KNOW I END UP HERE, IN THIS PARALLEL UNIVERSE
ALONE
ACTUALLY,
I HAVEN'T BEEN THAT LONELY
THESE GUYS ARE FOLLOWING MY EVERY MOVE
THEY GUIDE ME TOWARDS FOOD
THEY EVEN LIKE TO BE PET SOMETIMES

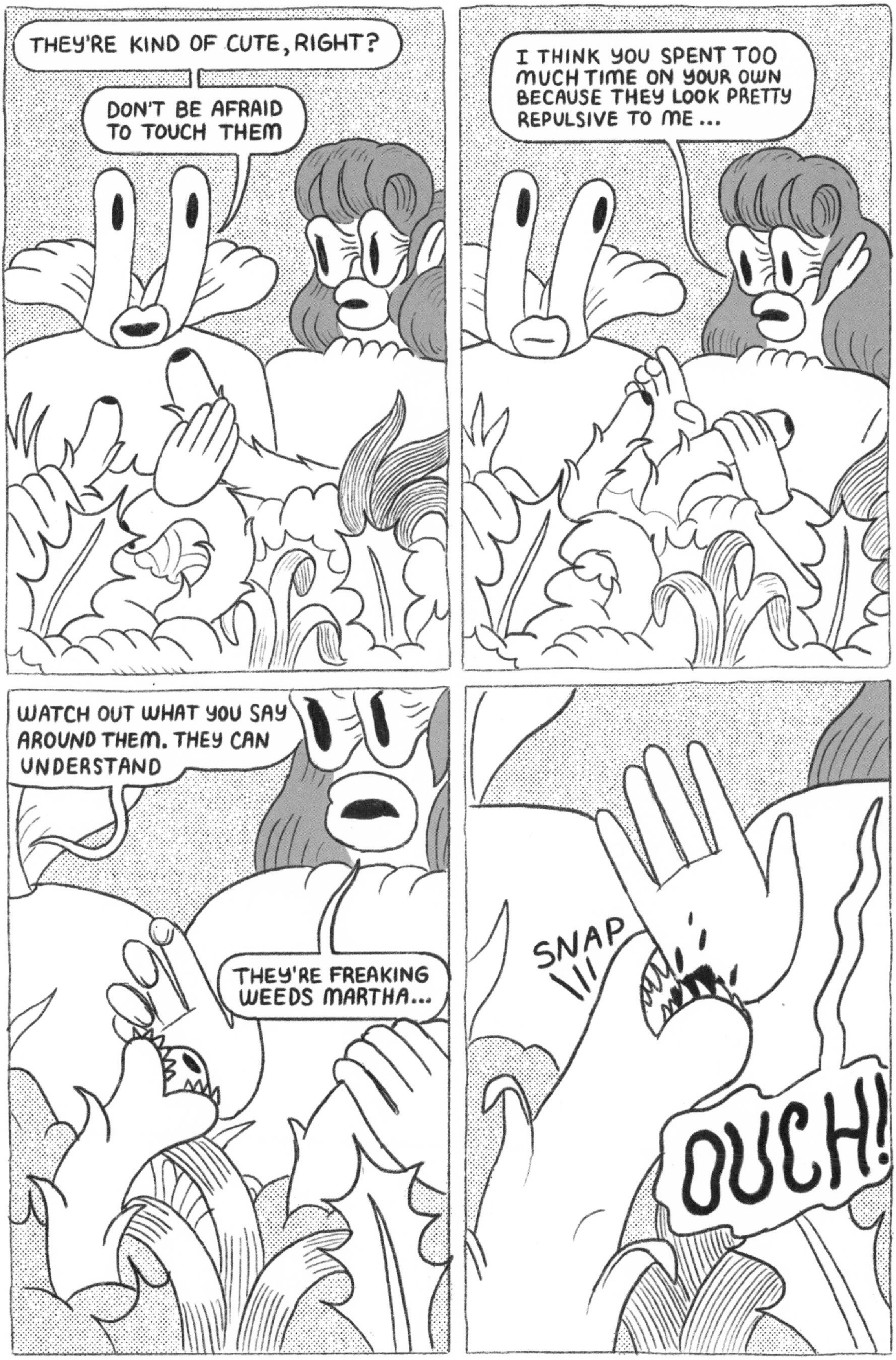
THEY'RE KIND OF CUTE, RIGHT?
DON'T BE AFRAID TO TOUCH THEM
I THINK YOU SPENT TOO MUCH TIME ON YOUR OWN BECAUSE THEY LOOK PRETTY REPULSIVE TO ME...
WATCH OUT WHAT YOU SAY AROUND THEM. THEY CAN UNDERSTAND
THEY'RE FREAKING WEEDS MARTHA...
SNAP
OUCH!

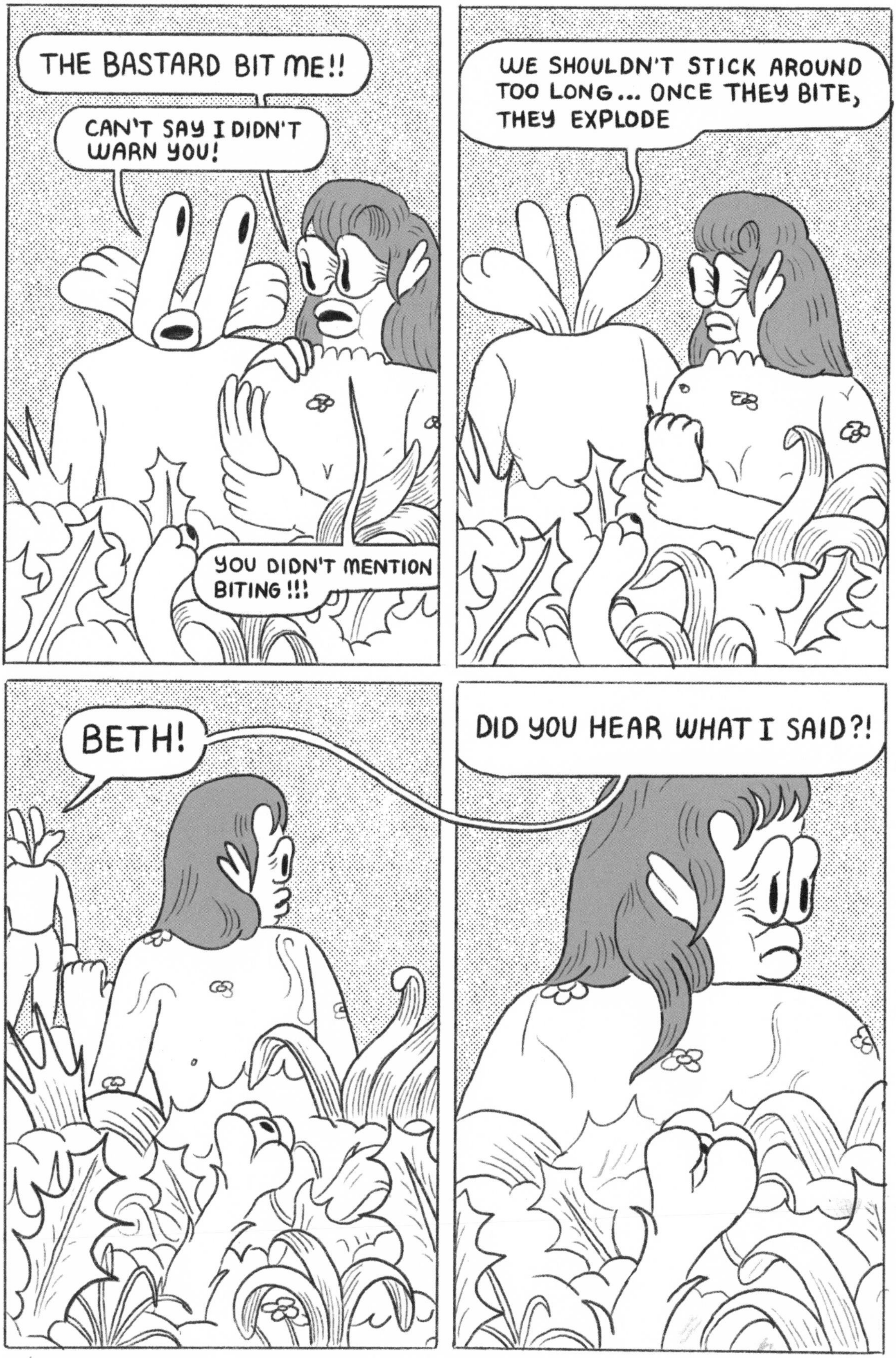
THE BASTARD BIT ME!!
CAN'T SAY I DIDN'T WARN YOU!
YOU DIDN'T MENTION BITING !!!
WE SHOULDN'T STICK AROUND TOO LONG... ONCE THEY BITE, THEY EXPLODE
BETH!
DID YOU HEAR WHAT I SAID?!

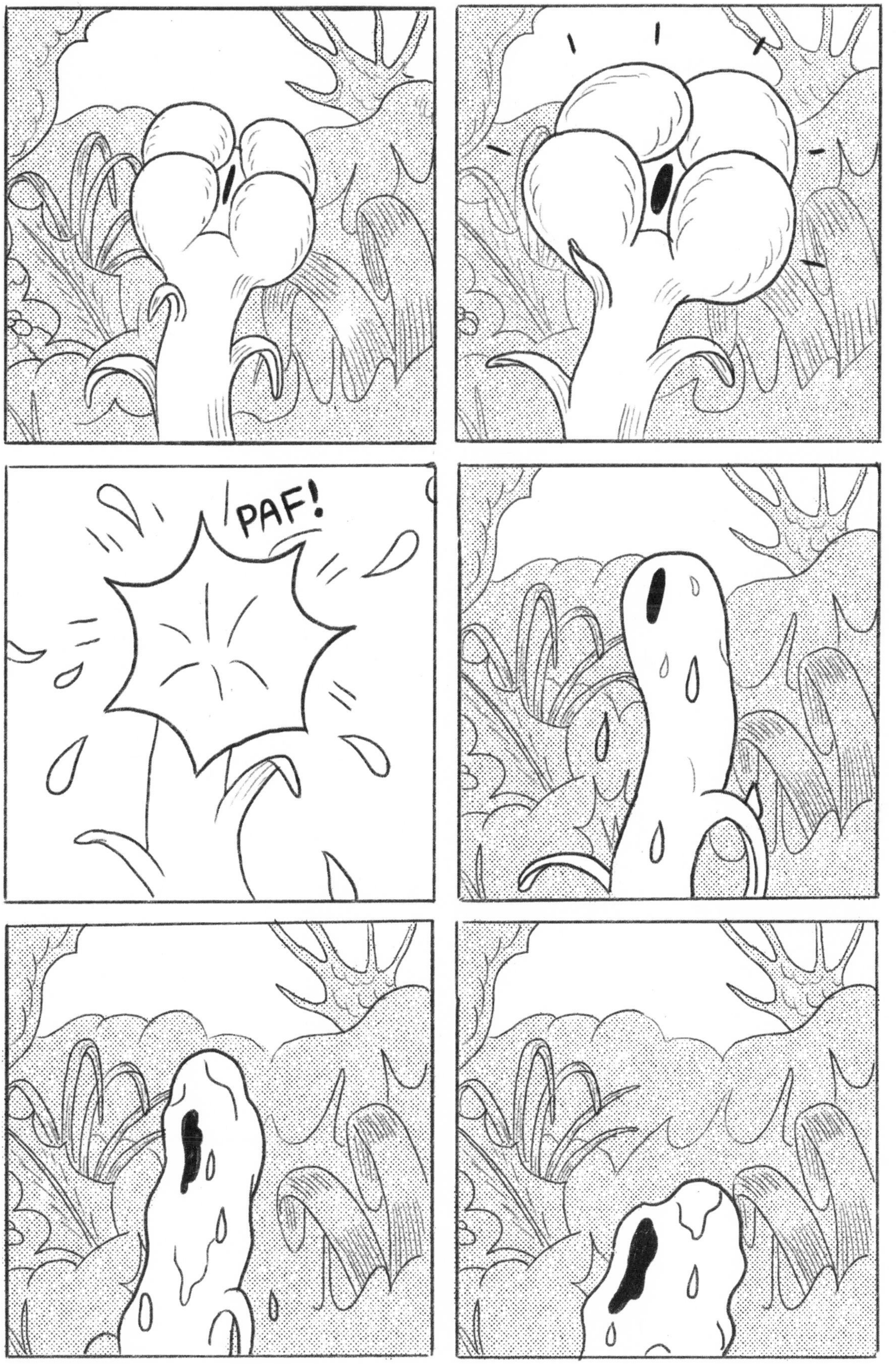
PAF!

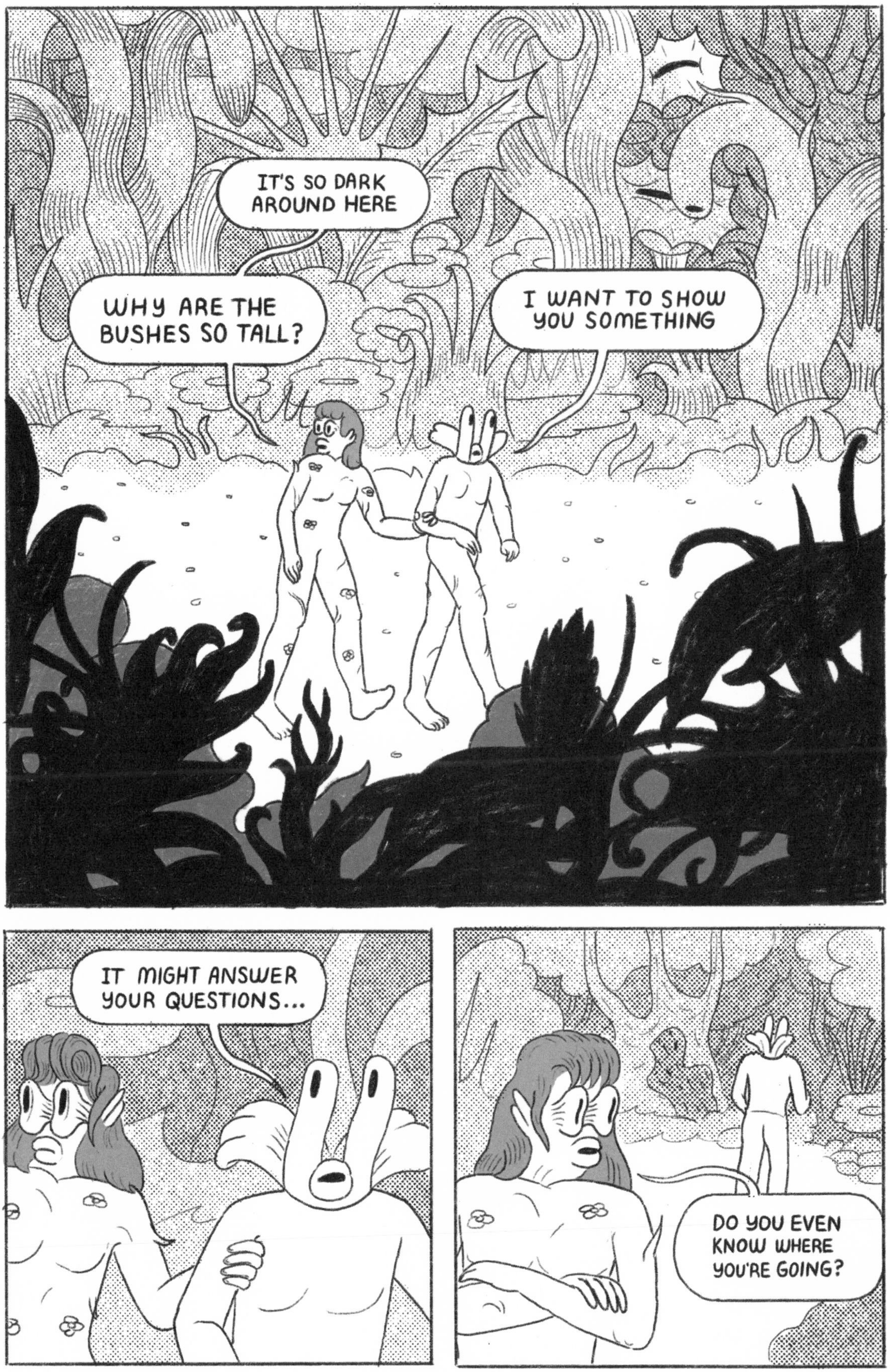
IT'S SO DARK AROUND HERE
WHY ARE THE BUSHES SO TALL?
I WANT TO SHOW YOU SOMETHING
IT MIGHT ANSWER YOUR QUESTIONS...
DO YOU EVEN KNOW WHERE YOU'RE GOING?

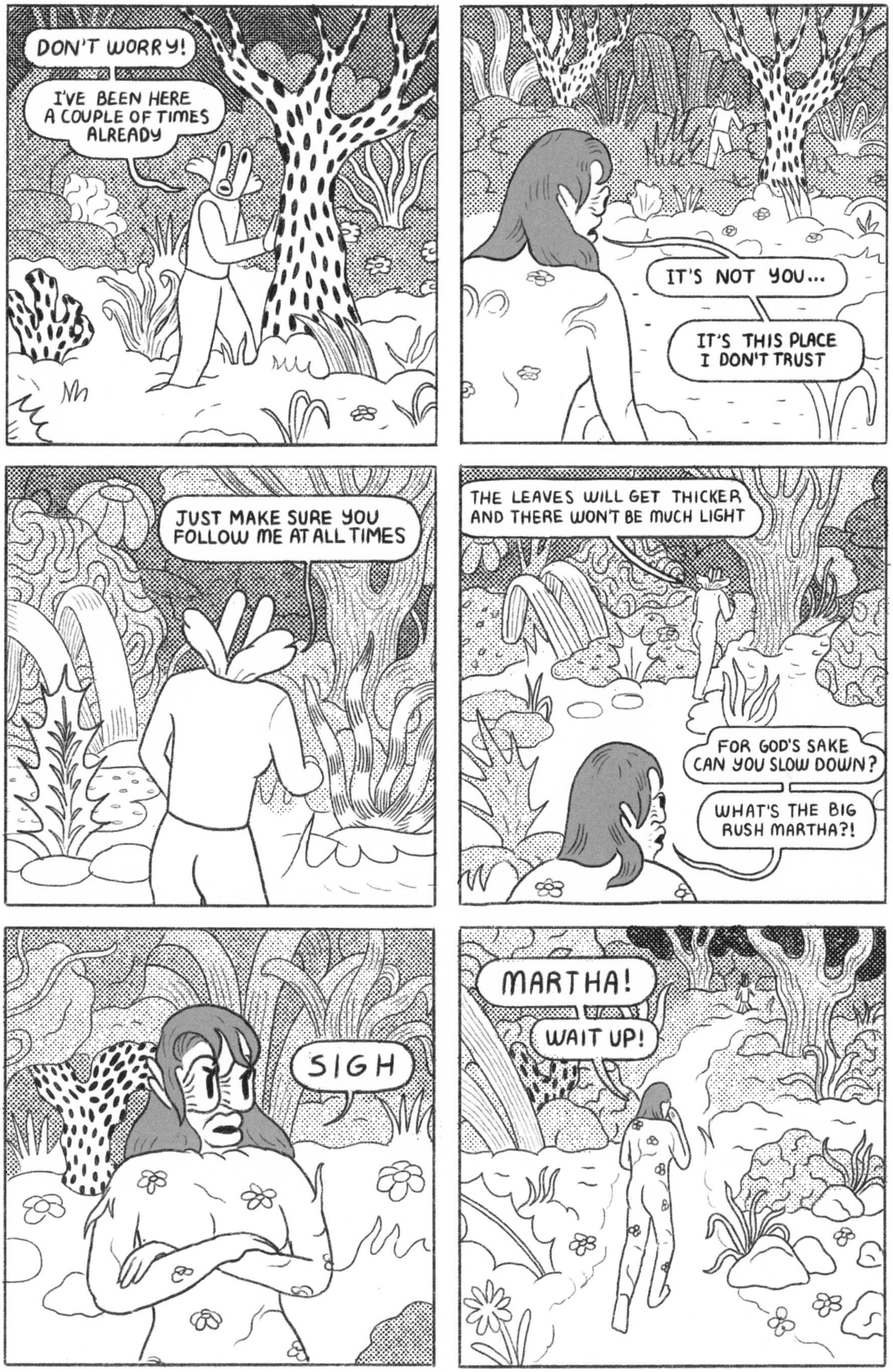
DON'T WORRY!
I'VE BEEN HERE A COUPLE OF TIMES ALREADY
IT'S NOT YOU...
IT'S THIS PLACE I DON'T TRUST
JUST MAKE SURE YOU FOLLOW ME AT ALL TIMES
THE LEAVES WILL GET THICKER AND THERE WON'T BE MUCH LIGHT
FOR GOD'S SAKE CAN YOU SLOW DOWN?
WHAT'S THE BIG RUSH MARTHA?!
SIGH
MARTHA!
WAIT UP!

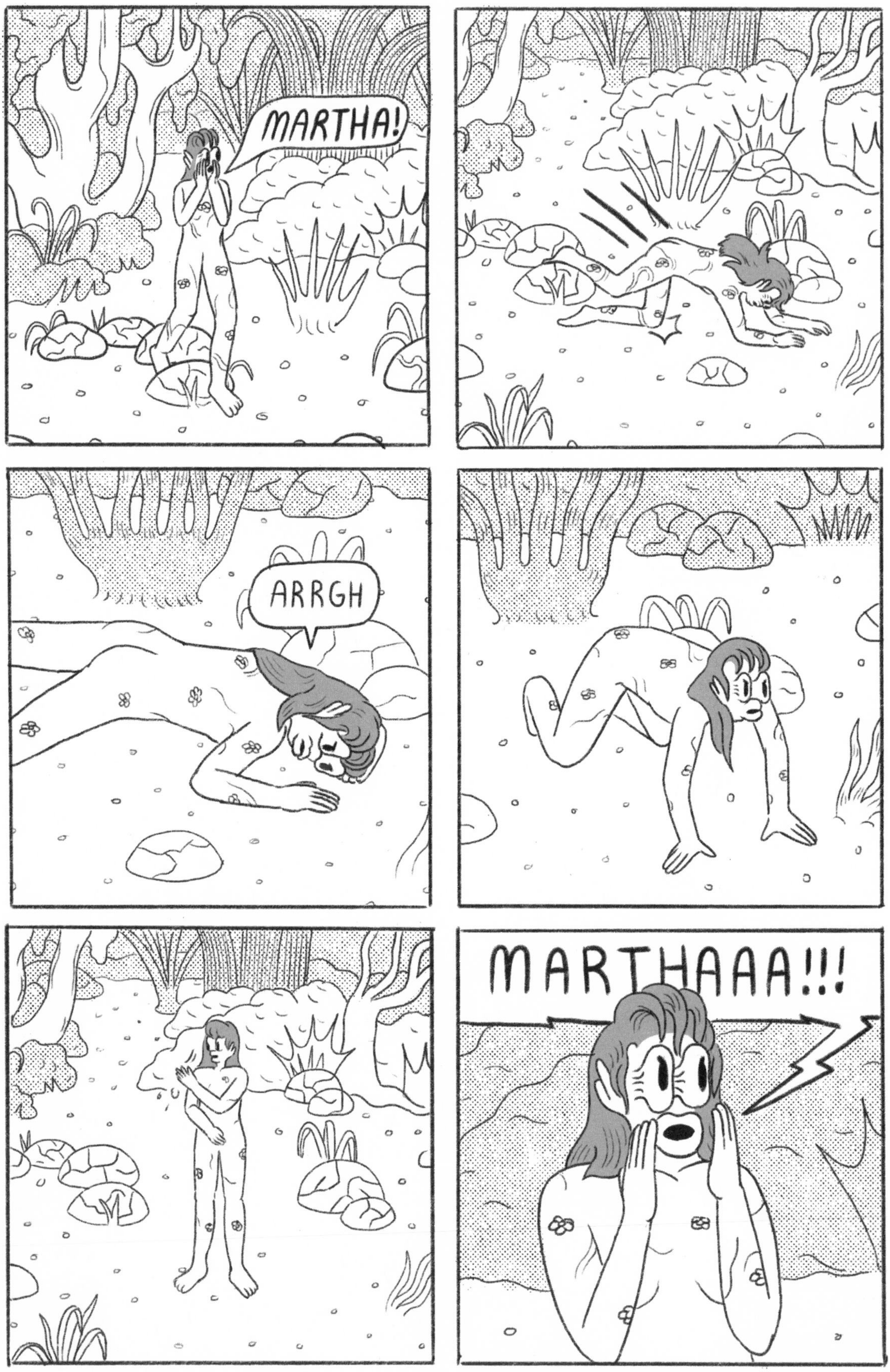
MARTHA!
ARRGH
MARTHAAA!!!

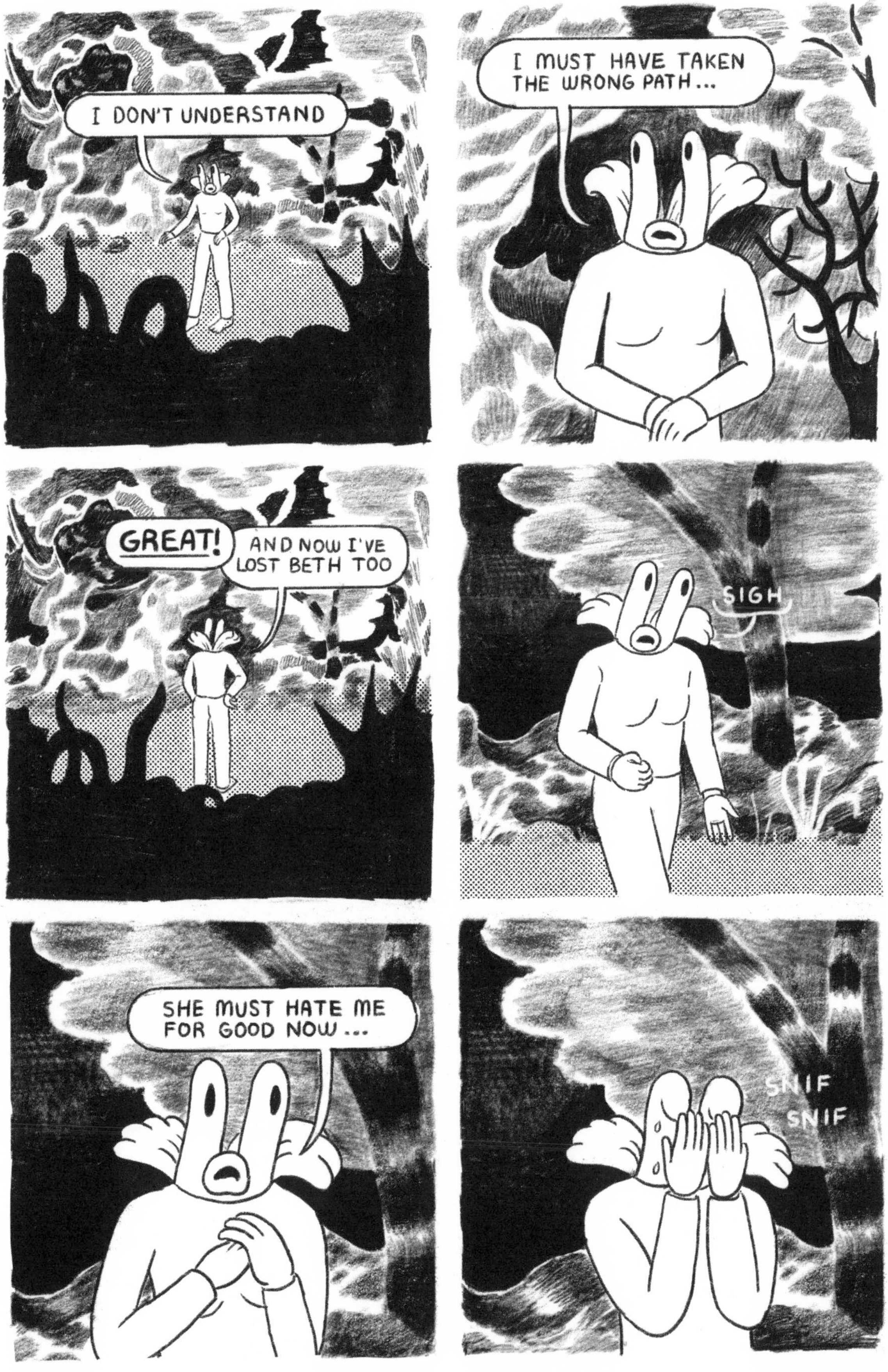
I DON'T UNDERSTAND
I MUST HAVE TAKEN THE WRONG PATH...
GREAT!
AND NOW I'VE LOST BETH TOO
SIGH
SHE MUST HATE ME FOR GOOD NOW...
SNIF
SNIF

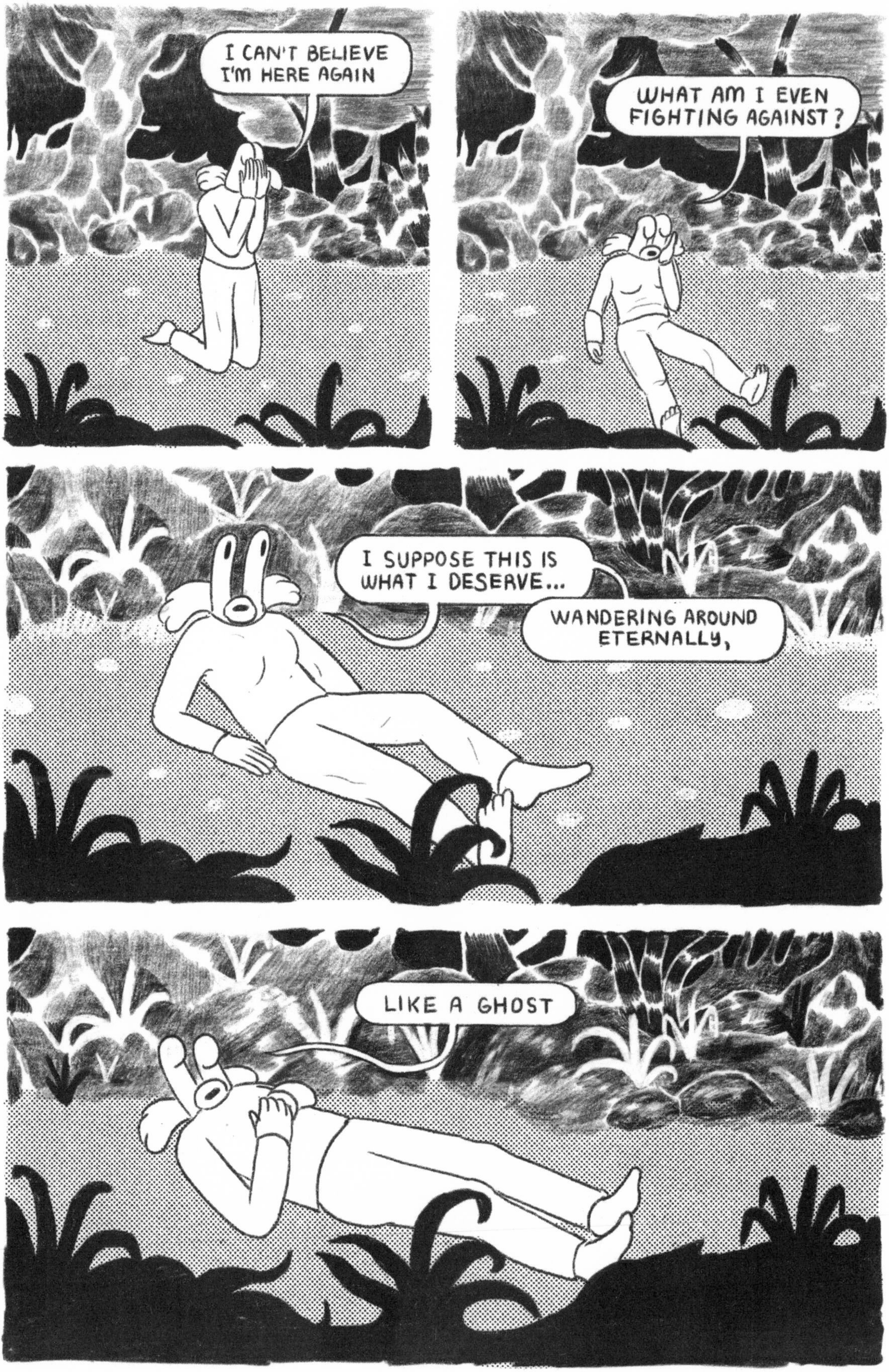
I CAN'T BELIEVE I'M HERE AGAIN
WHAT AM I EVEN FIGHTING AGAINST?
I SUPPOSE THIS IS WHAT I DESERVE...
WANDERING AROUND ETERNALLY,
LIKE A GHOST

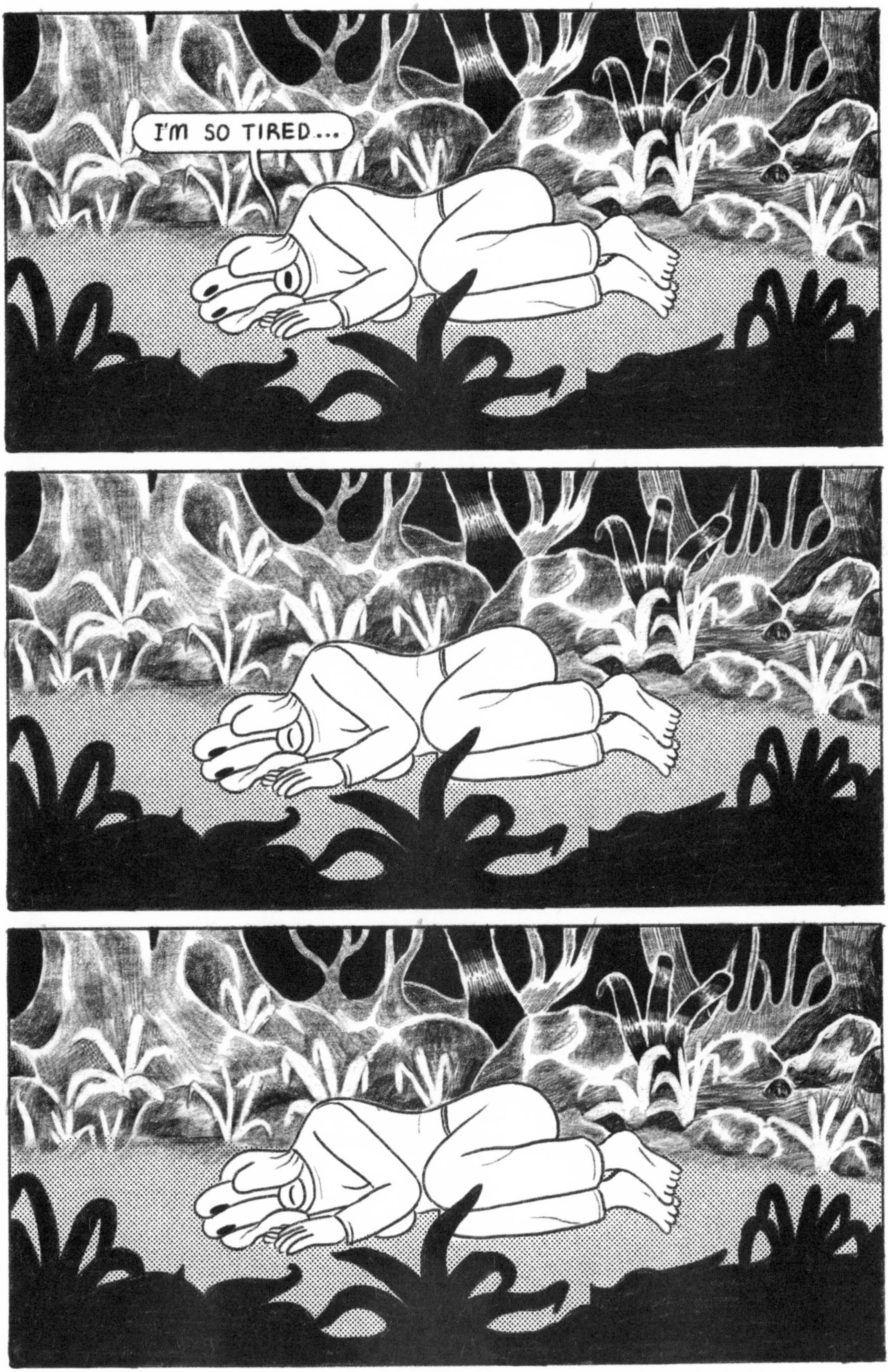
I'M SO TIRED....

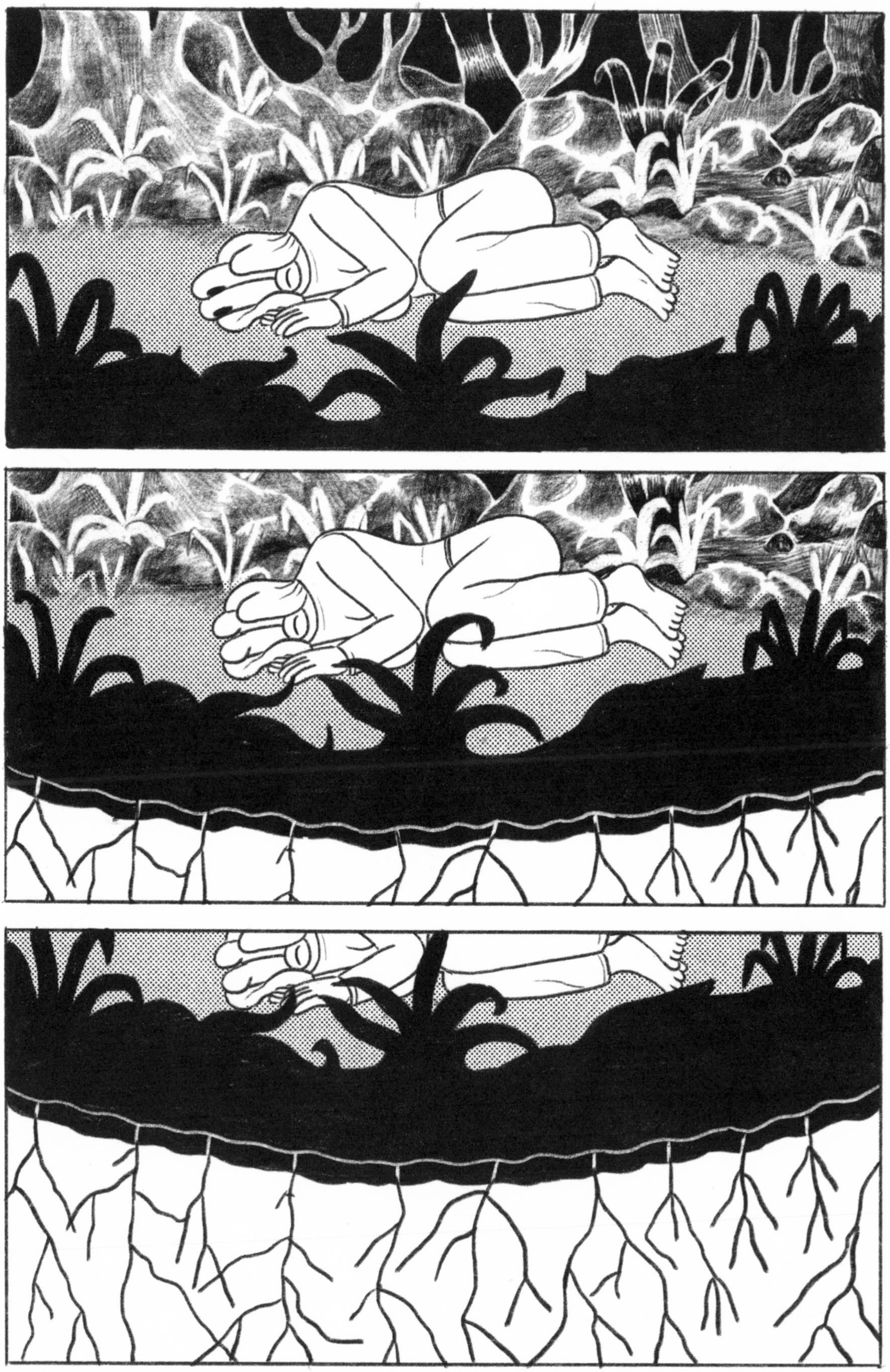

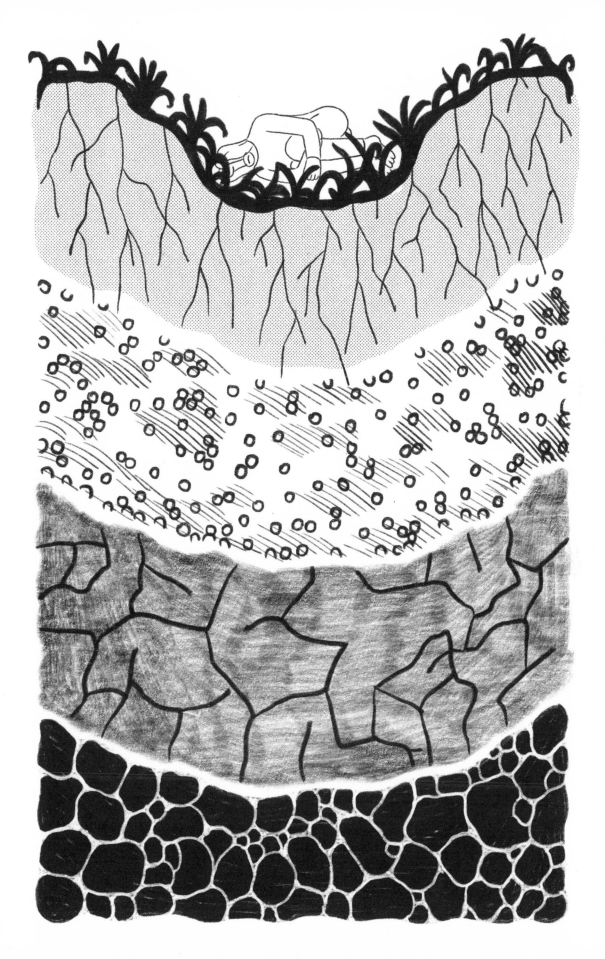

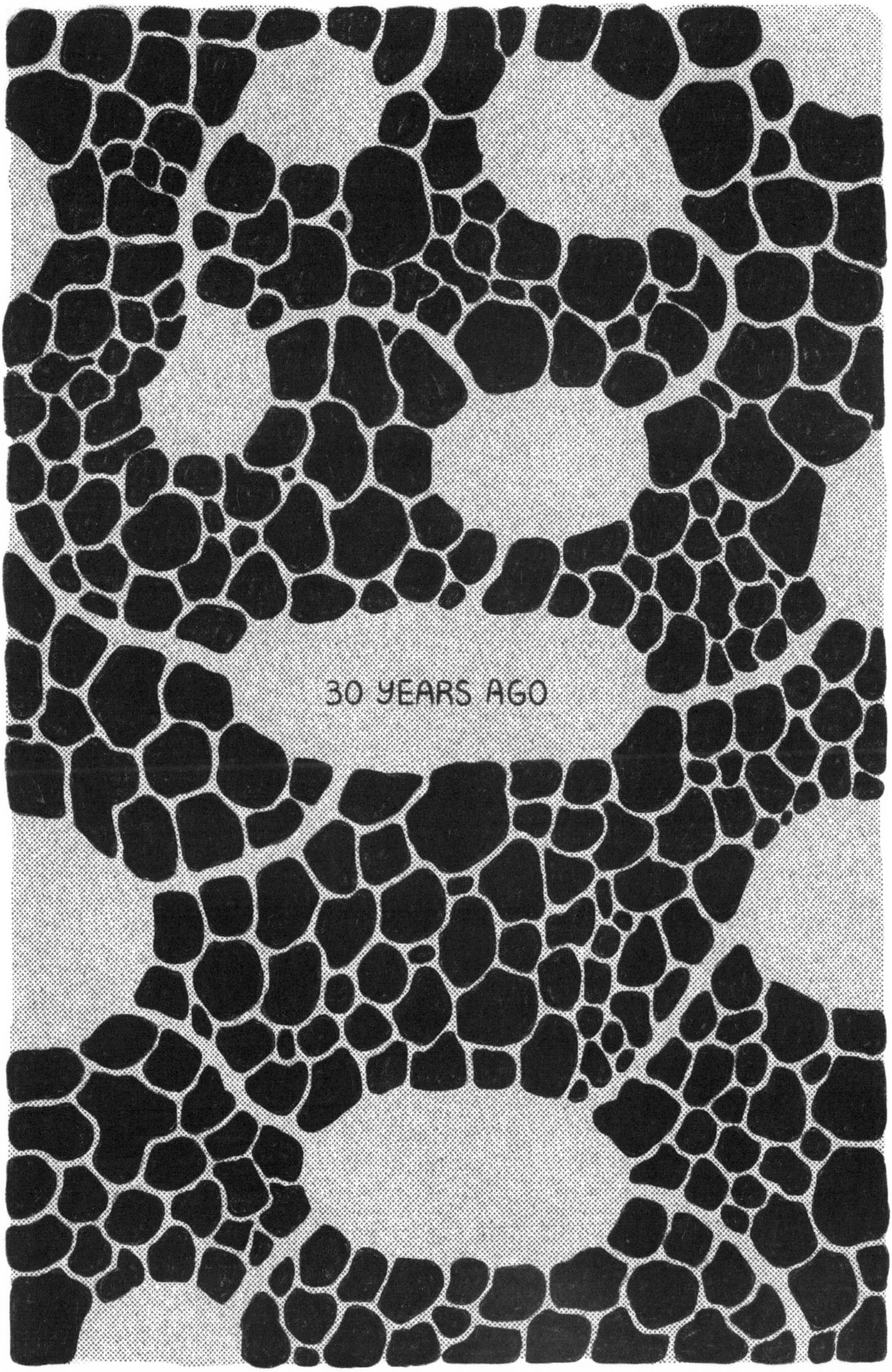
30 YEARS AGO

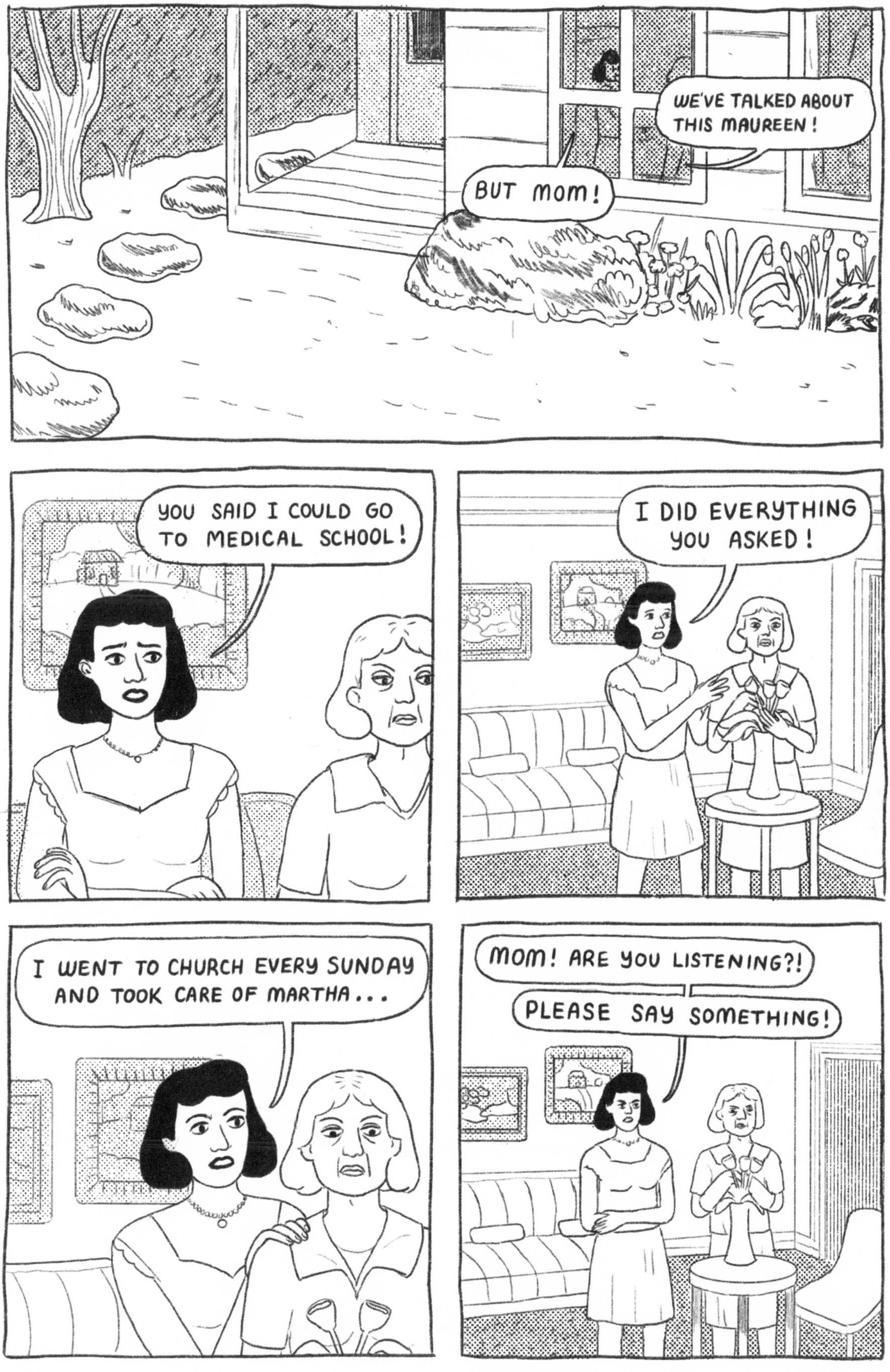
WE'VE TALKED ABOUT THIS MAUREEN!
BUT MOM!
YOU SAID I COULD GO TO MEDICAL SCHOOL!
I DID EVERYTHING YOU ASKED!
I WENT TO CHURCH EVERY SUNDAY AND TOOK CARE OF MARTHA...
MOM! ARE YOU LISTENING?!
PLEASE SAY SOMETHING!

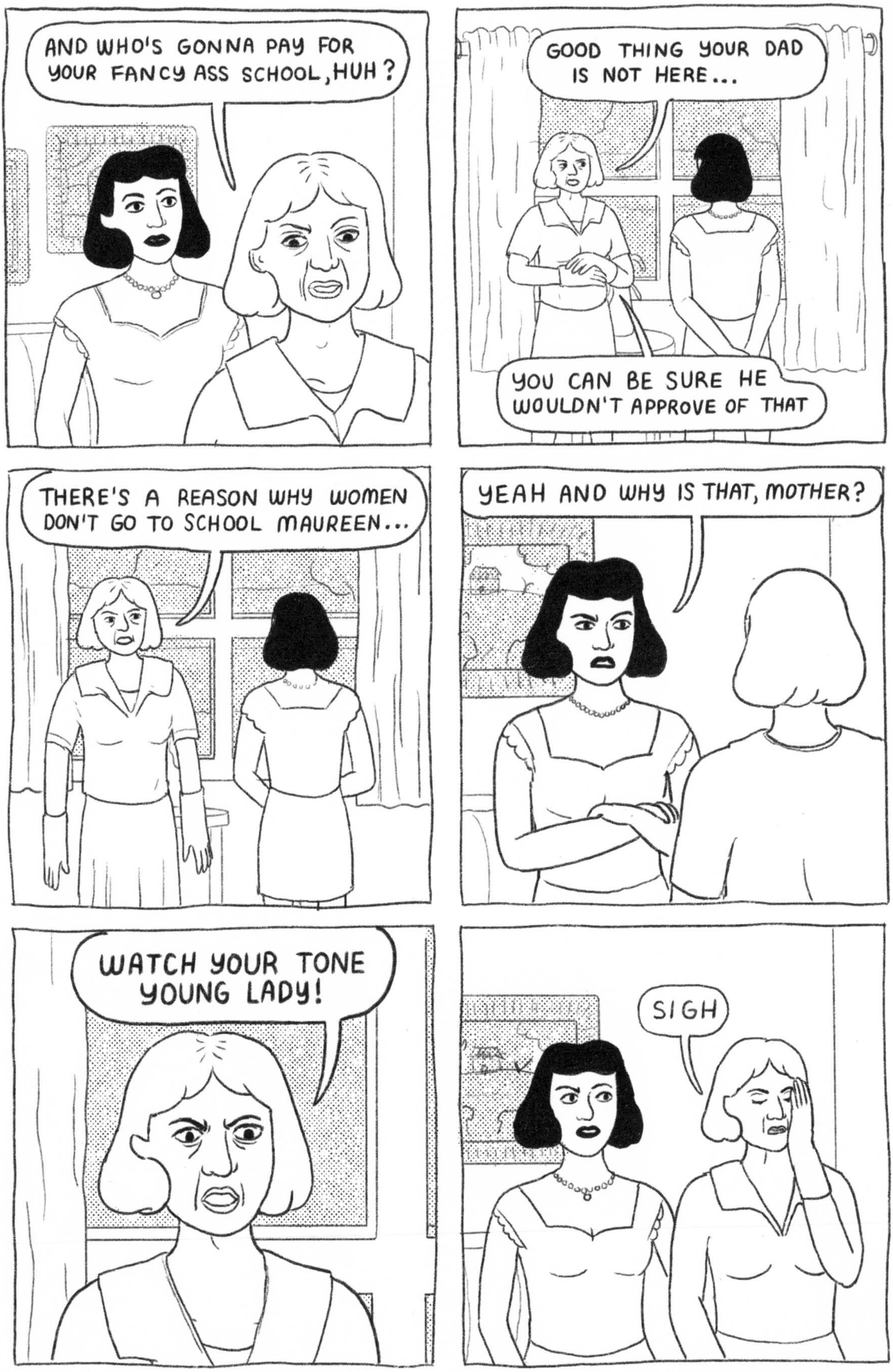
AND WHO'S GONNA PAY FOR YOUR FANCY ASS SCHOOL, HUH?
GOOD THING YOUR DAD IS NOT HERE...
YOU CAN BE SURE HE WOULDN'T APPROVE OF THAT
THERE'S A REASON WHY WOMEN DON'T GO TO SCHOOL MAUREEN...
YEAH AND WHY IS THAT, MOTHER?
WATCH YOUR TONE YOUNG LADY!
SIGH

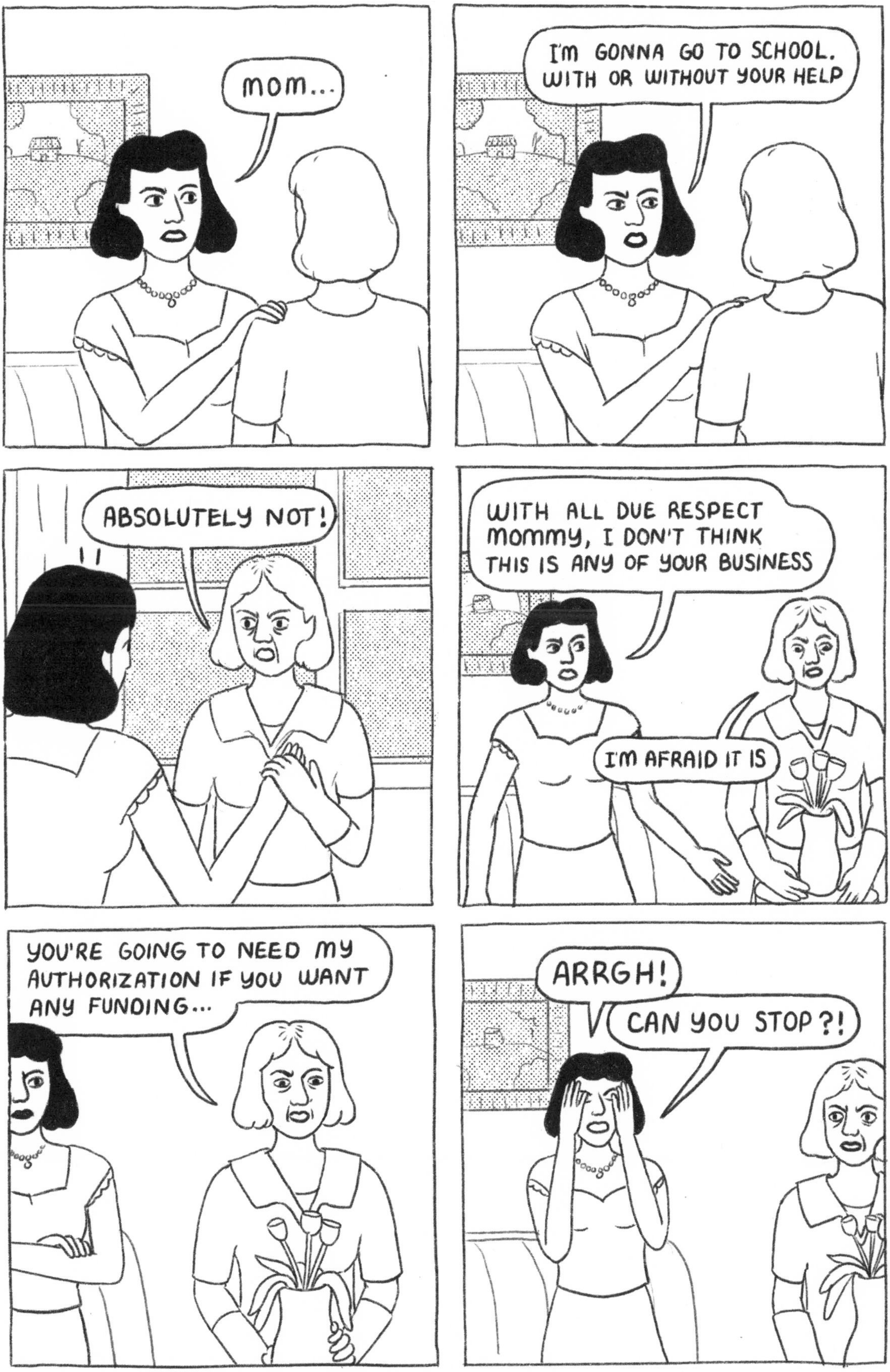
MOM...
I'M GONNA GO TO SCHOOL. WITH OR WITHOUT YOUR HELP
ABSOLUTELY NOT!
WITH ALL DUE RESPECT MOMMY, I DON'T THINK THIS IS ANY OF YOUR BUSINESS
I'M AFRAID IT IS
YOU'RE GOING TO NEED MY AUTHORIZATION IF YOU WANT ANY FUNDING...
ARRGH!
CAN YOU STOP?!

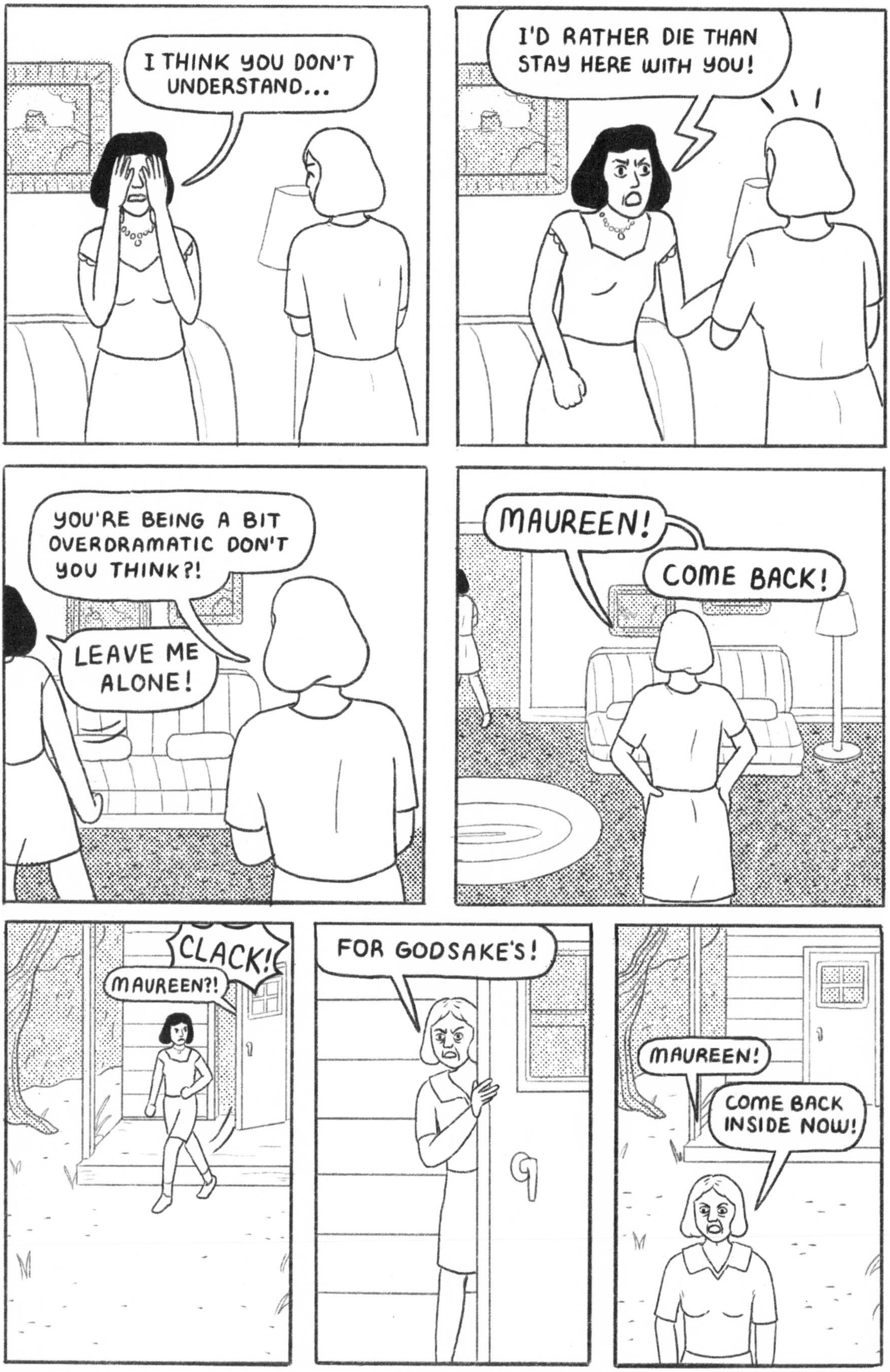
I THINK YOU DON'T UNDERSTAND...
I'D RATHER DIE THAN STAY HERE WITH YOU!
YOU'RE BEING A BIT OVERDRAMATIC DON'T YOU THINK?!
LEAVE ME ALONE!
MAUREEN!
COME BACK!
CLACK!
MAUREEN?!
FOR GODSAKE'S!
MAUREEN!
COME BACK INSIDE NOW!

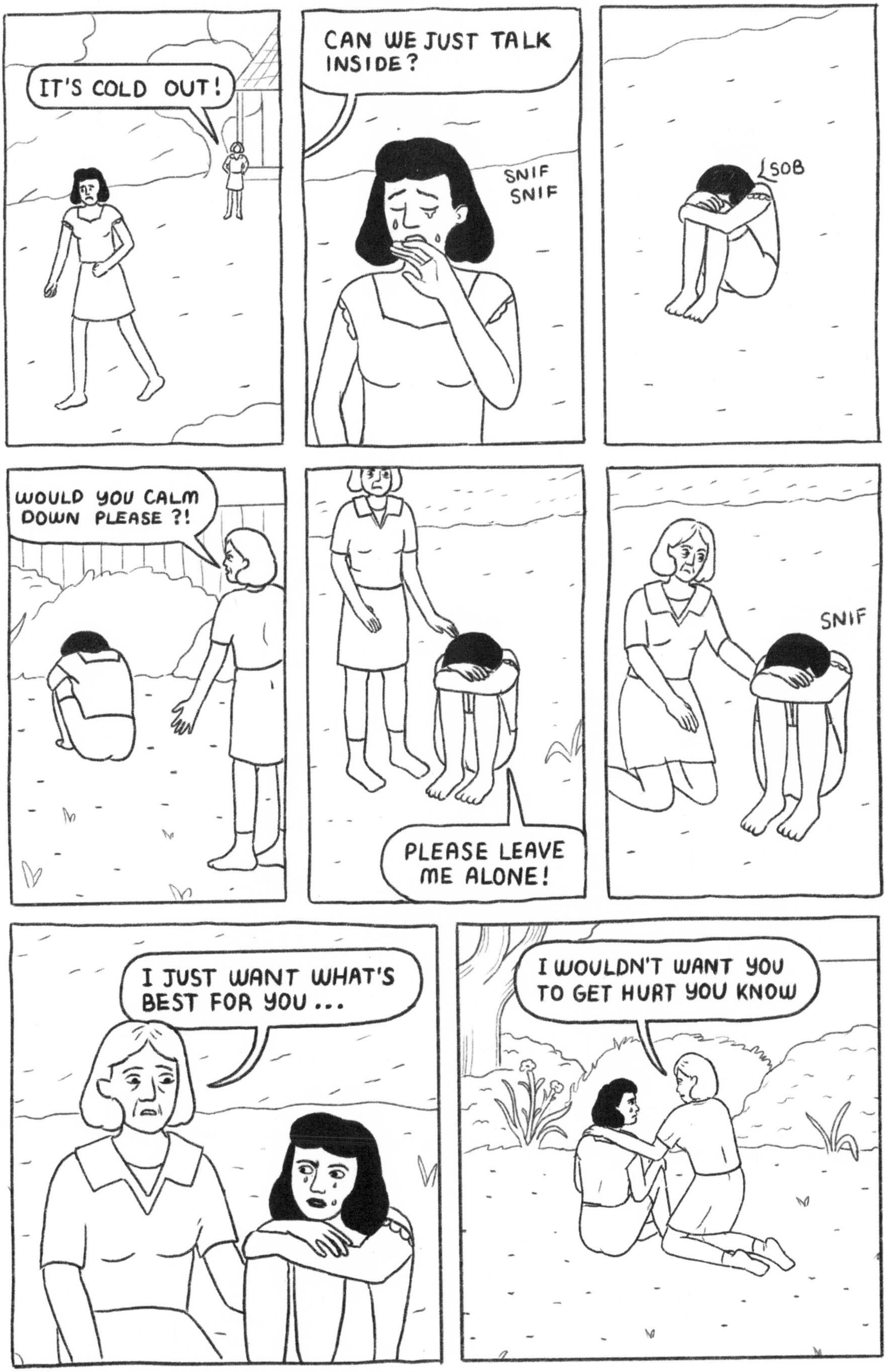
IT'S COLD OUT!
CAN WE JUST TALK INSIDE?
SNIF SNIF
SOB
WOULD YOU CALM DOWN PLEASE ?!
PLEASE LEAVE ME ALONE!
SNIF
I JUST WANT WHAT'S BEST FOR YOU ...
I WOULDN'T WANT YOU TO GET HURT YOU KNOW

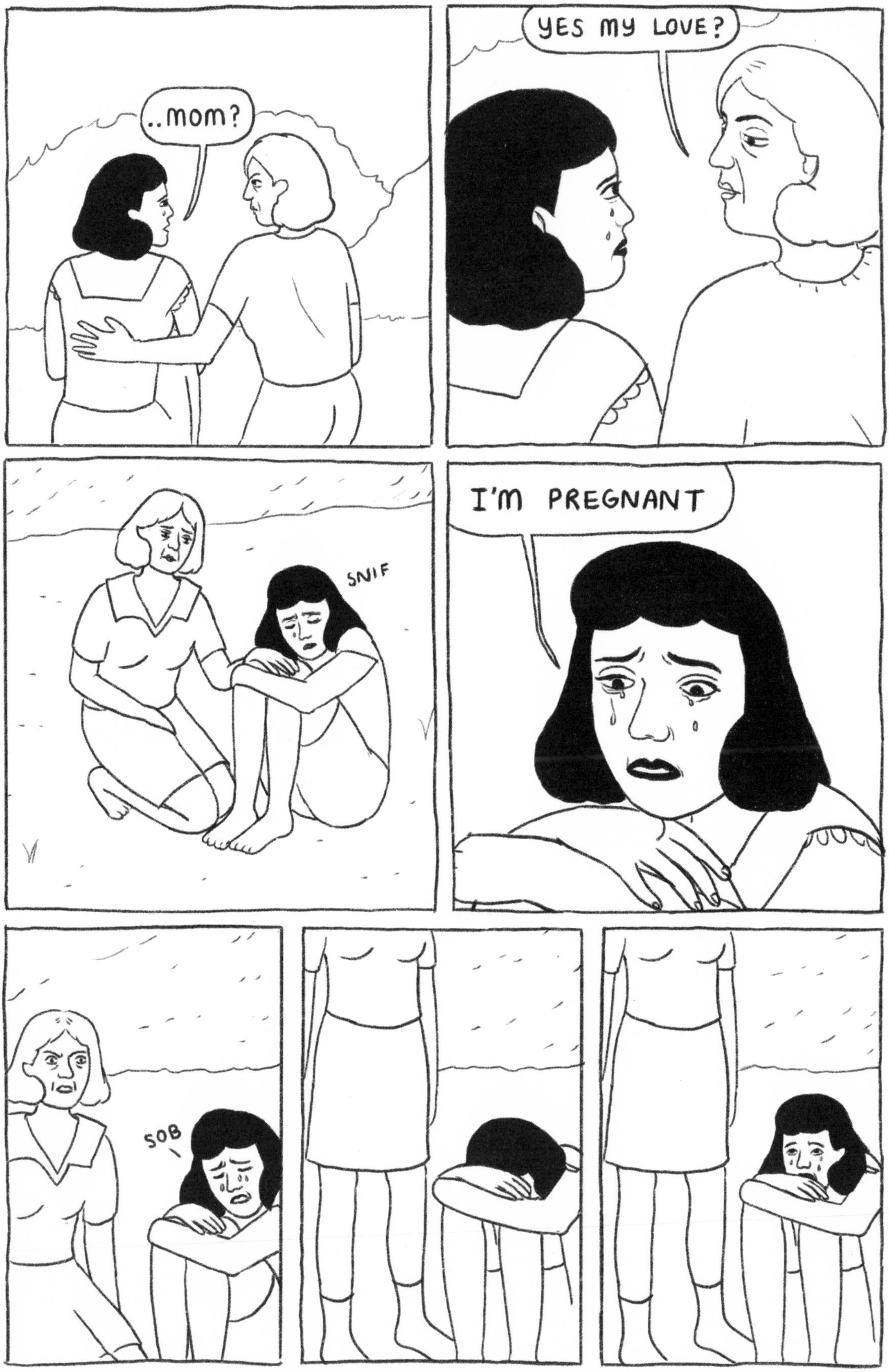
..mom?
YES MY LOVE?
SNIF
I'M PREGNANT
SOB

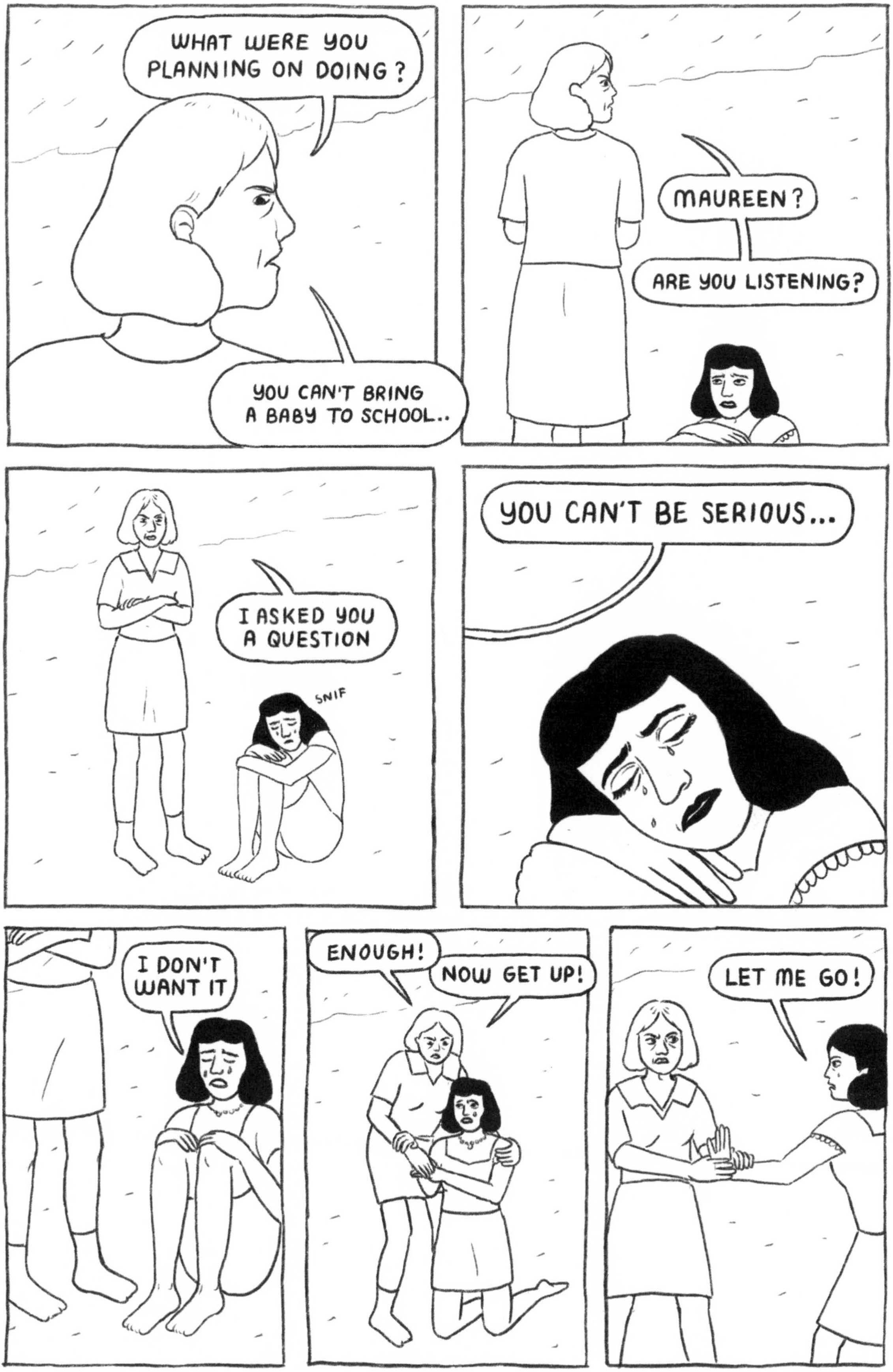
WHAT WERE YOU PLANNING ON DOING?
YOU CAN'T BRING A BABY TO SCHOOL..
MAUREEN?
ARE YOU LISTENING?
I ASKED YOU A QUESTION
SNIF
YOU CAN'T BE SERIOUS...
I DON'T WANT IT
ENOUGH!
NOW GET UP!
LET ME GO!

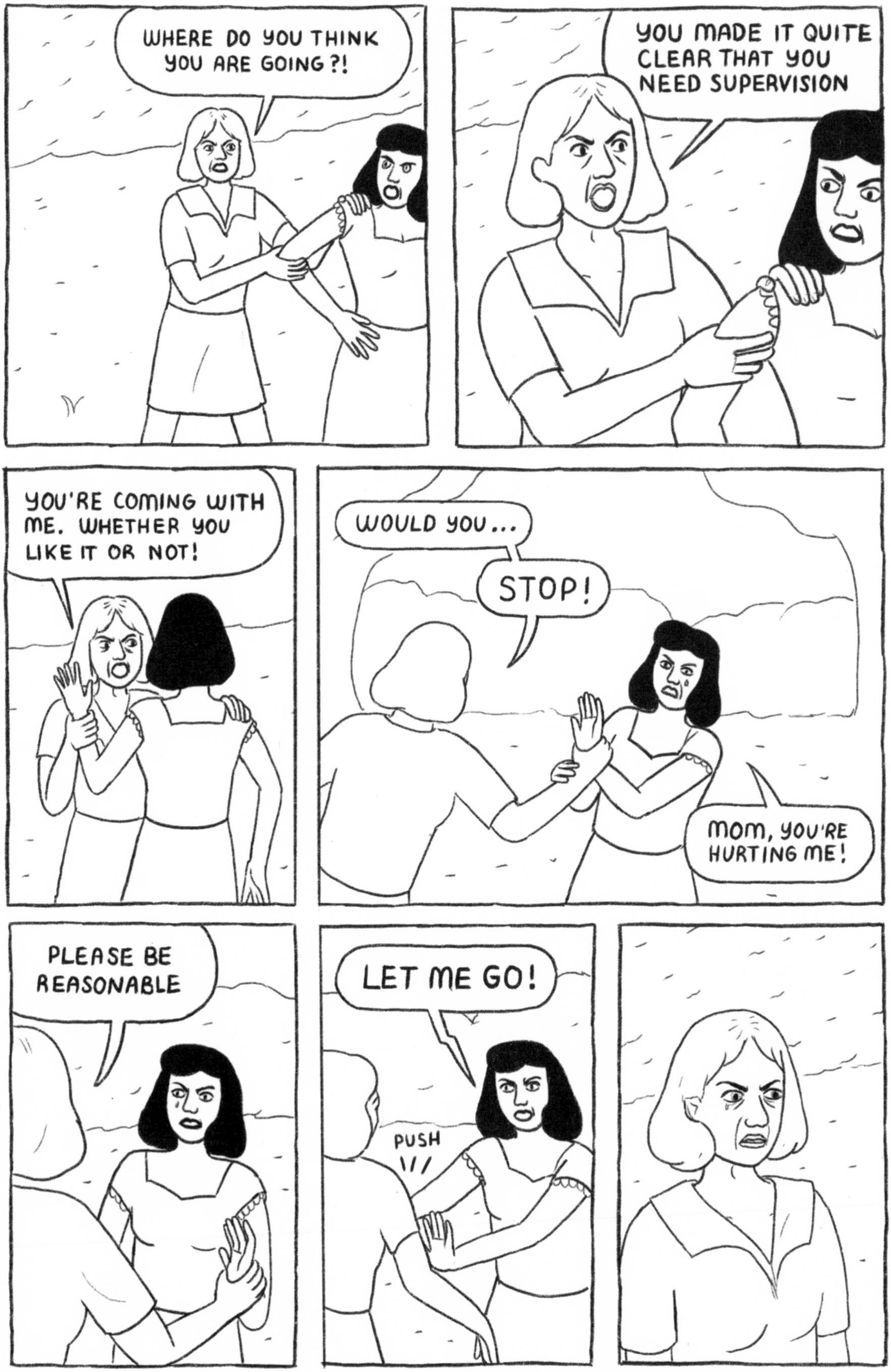
WHERE DO YOU THINK YOU ARE GOING?!
YOU MADE IT QUITE CLEAR THAT YOU NEED SUPERVISION
YOU'RE COMING WITH ME. WHETHER YOU LIKE IT OR NOT!
WOULD YOU...
STOP!
MOM, YOU'RE HURTING ME!
PLEASE BE REASONABLE
LET ME GO!
PUSH

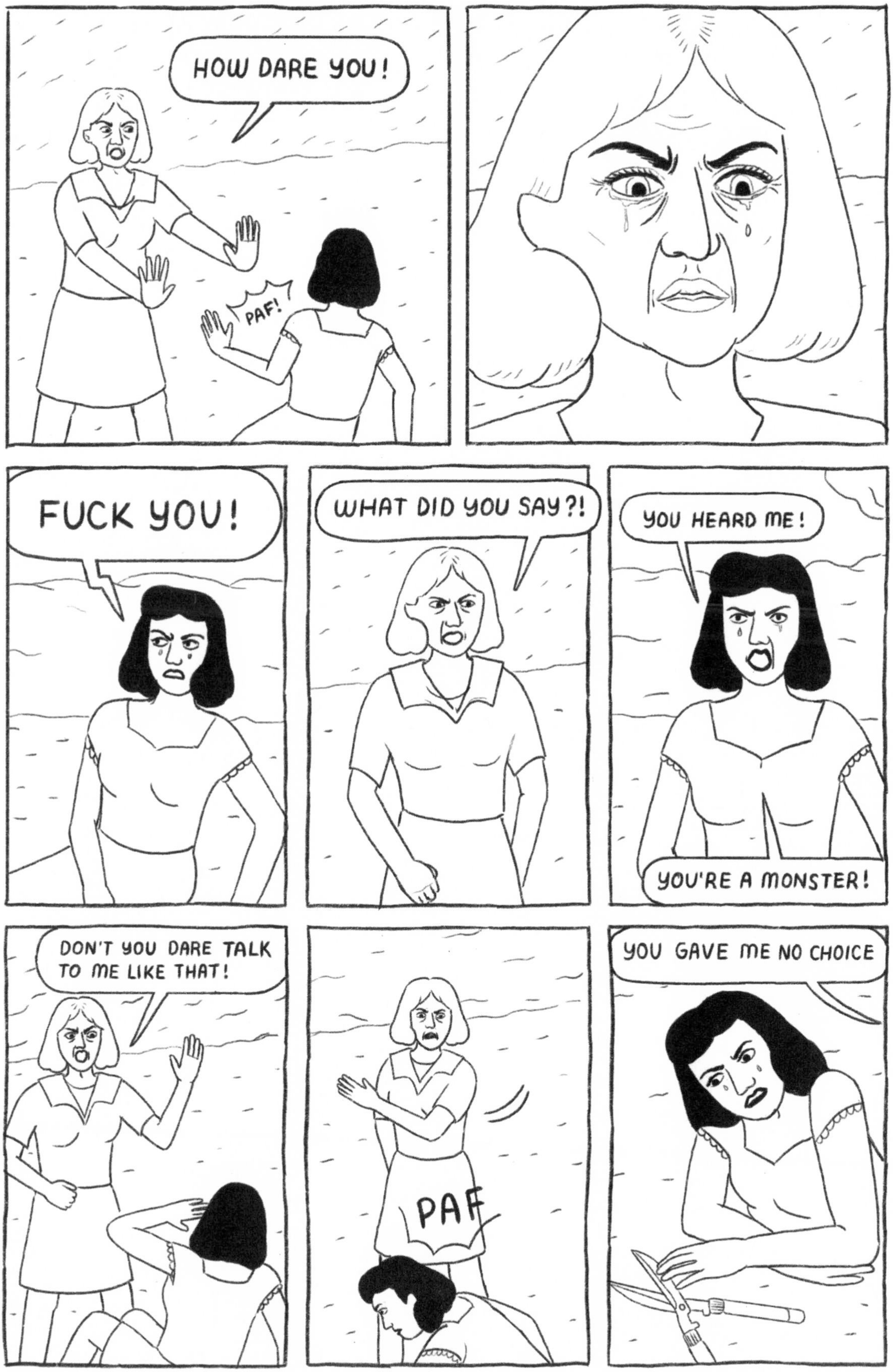
HOW DARE YOU!
PAF!
FUCK YOU!
WHAT DID YOU SAY?!
YOU HEARD ME!
YOU'RE A MONSTER!
DON'T YOU DARE TALK TO ME LIKE THAT!
PAF
YOU GAVE ME NO CHOICE

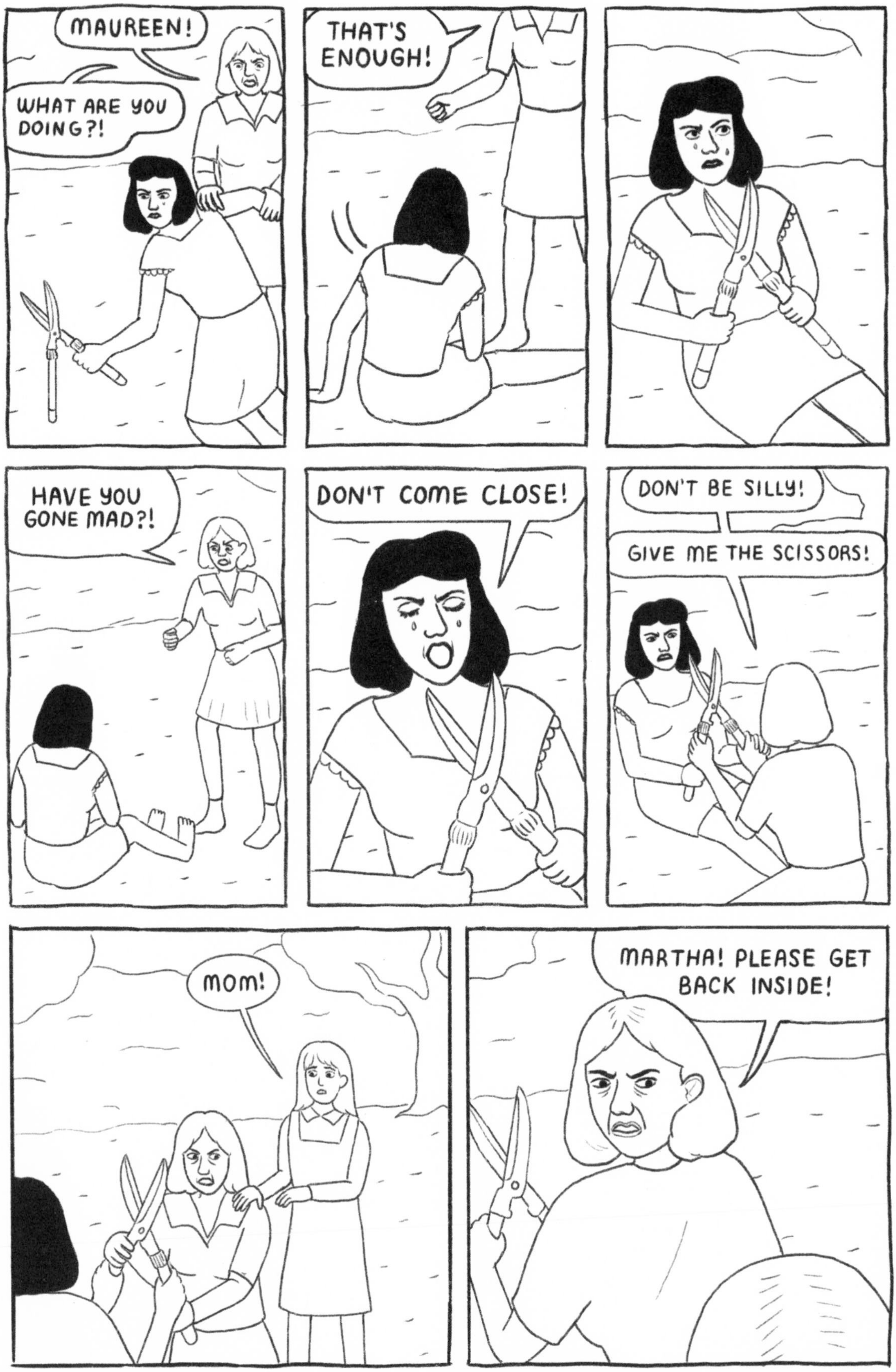
MAUREEN!
WHAT ARE YOU DOING?!
THAT'S ENOUGH!
HAVE YOU GONE MAD?!
DON'T COME CLOSE!
DON'T BE SILLY!
GIVE ME THE SCISSORS!
MOM!
MARTHA! PLEASE GET BACK INSIDE!

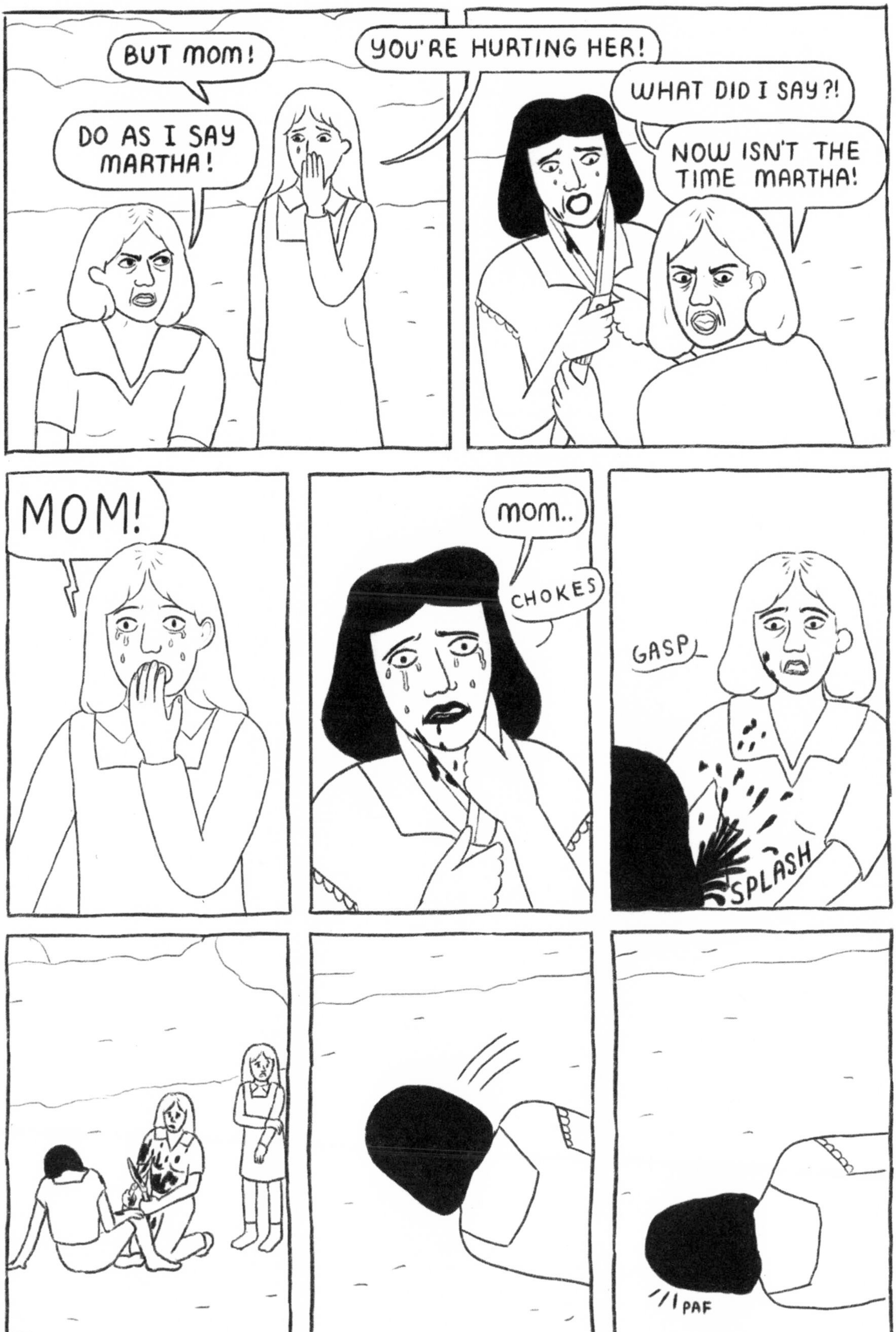
BUT mom!
DO AS I SAY MARTHA!
YOU'RE HURTING HER!
WHAT DID I SAY?!
NOW ISN'T THE TIME MARTHA!
MOM!
mom..
CHOKES
GASP
SPLASH
PAF

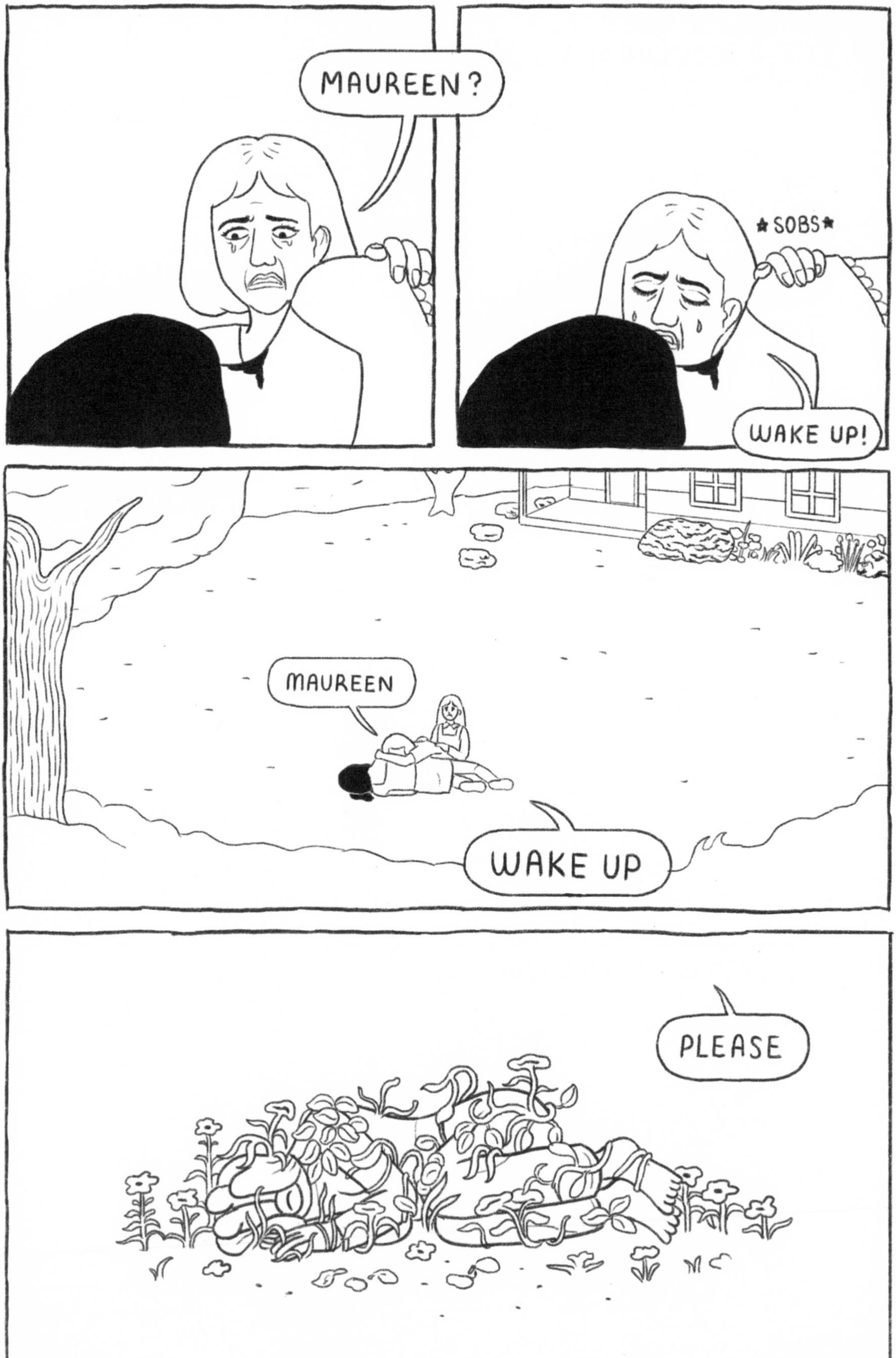
MAUREEN?
SOBS
WAKE UP!
MAUREEN
WAKE UP
PLEASE

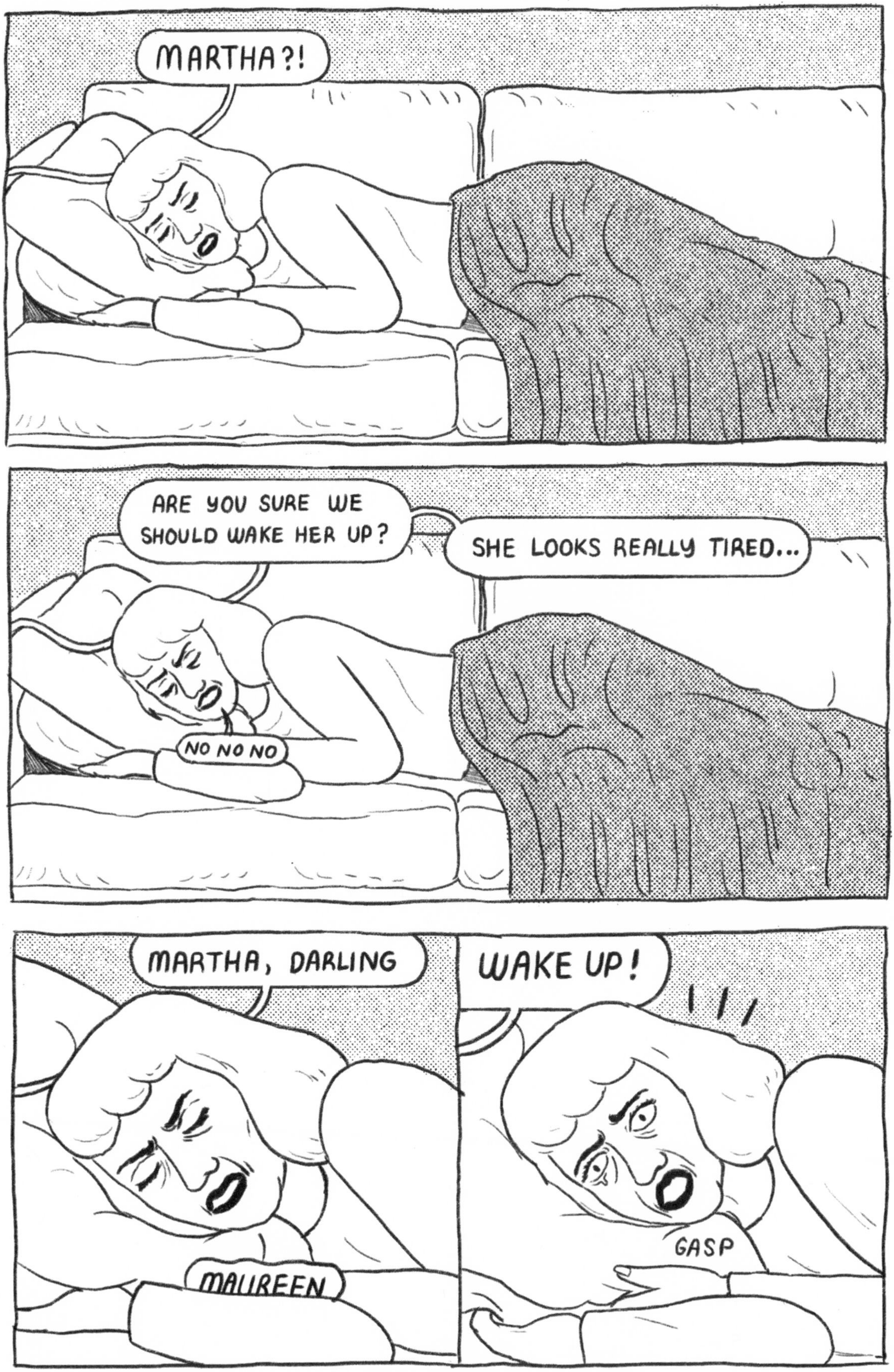
MARTHA?!
ARE YOU SURE WE SHOULD WAKE HER UP?
SHE LOOKS REALLY TIRED...
NO NO NO
MARTHA, DARLING
MAUREEN
WAKE UP!
GASP

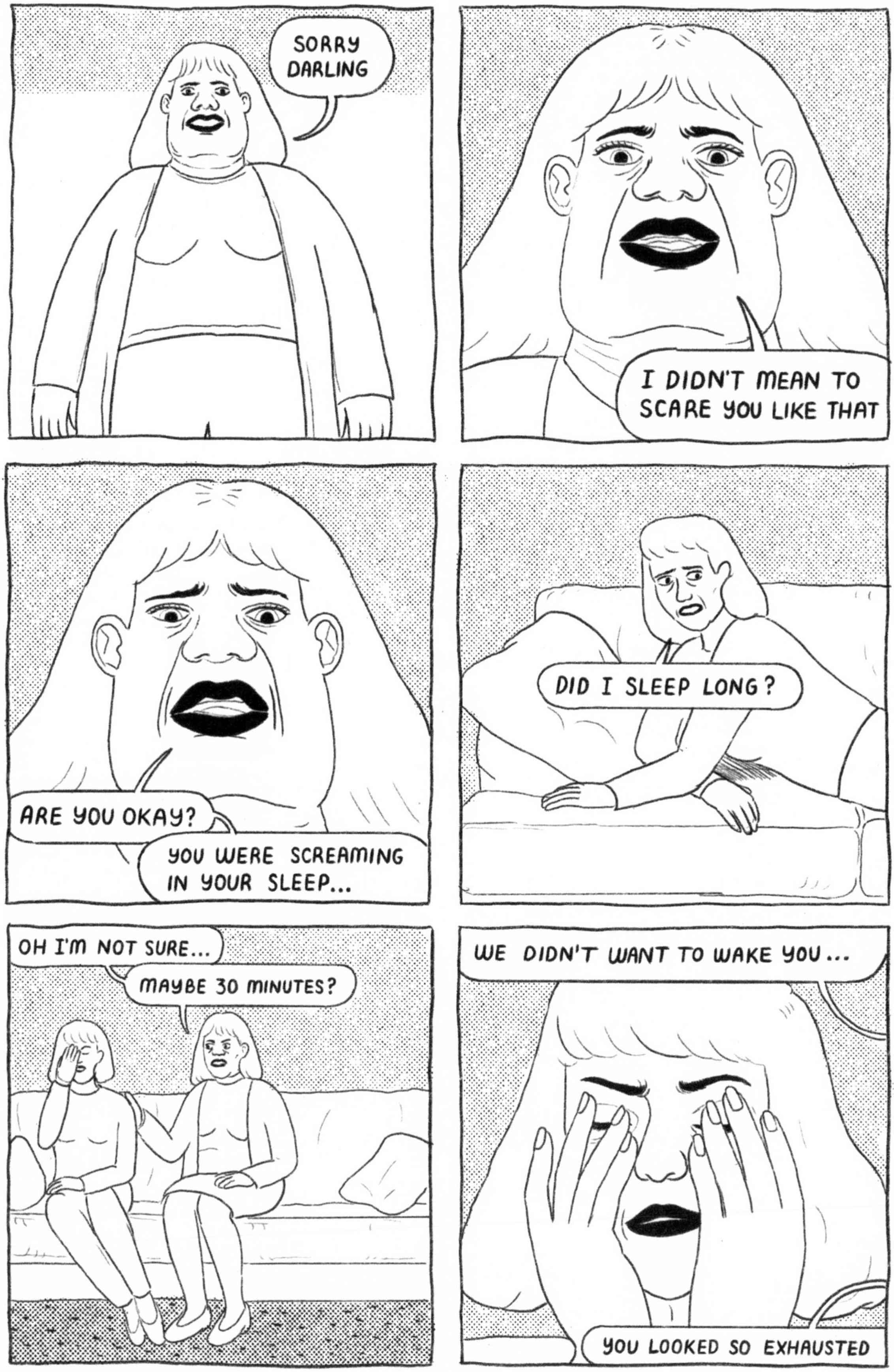
SORRY DARLING
I DIDN'T MEAN TO SCARE YOU LIKE THAT
ARE YOU OKAY?
YOU WERE SCREAMING IN YOUR SLEEP...
DID I SLEEP LONG?
OH I'M NOT SURE...
MAYBE 30 MINUTES?
WE DIDN'T WANT TO WAKE YOU...
YOU LOOKED SO EXHAUSTED

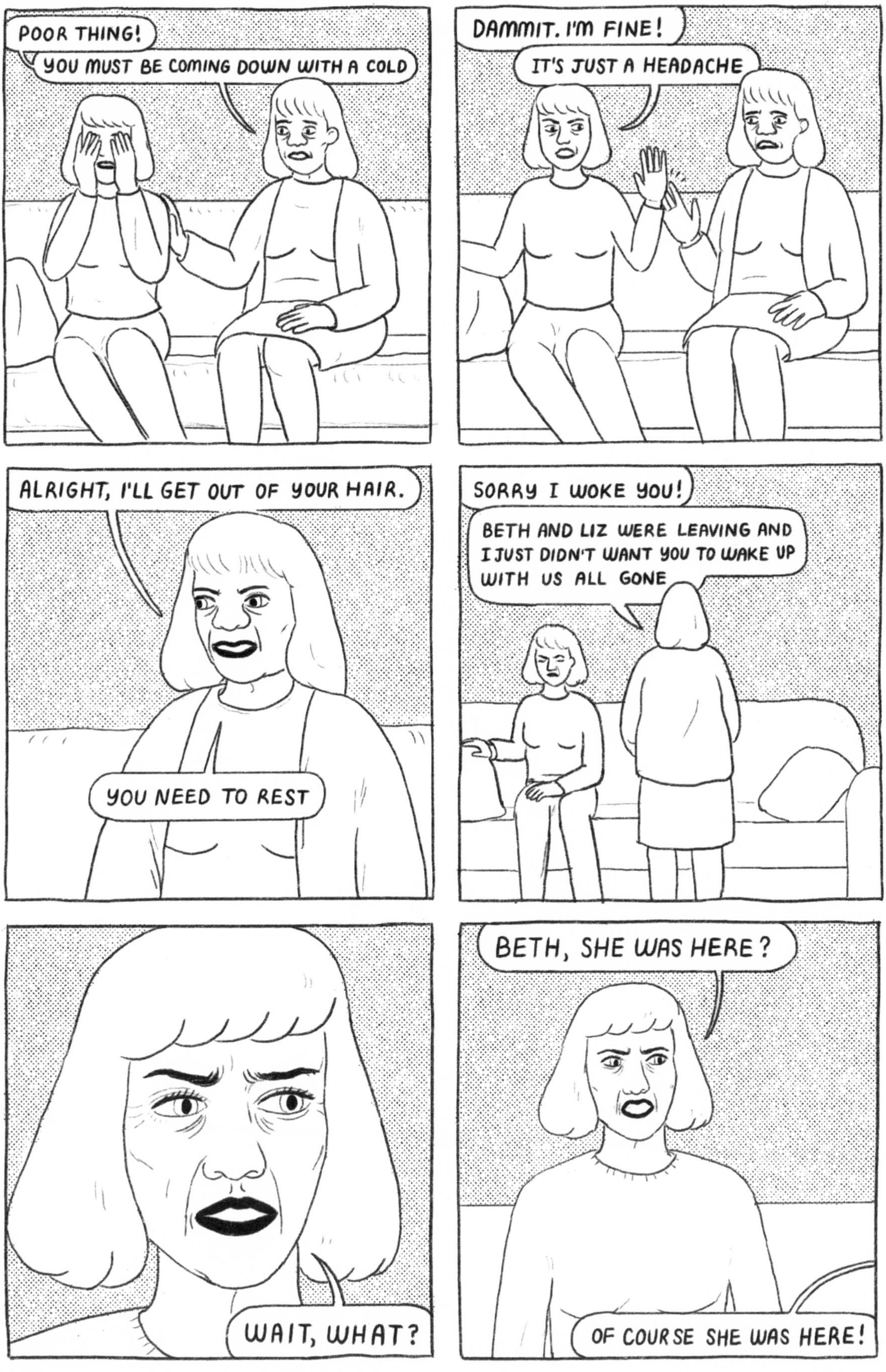
POOR THING!
YOU MUST BE COMING DOWN WITH A COLD
DAMMIT. I'M FINE!
IT'S JUST A HEADACHE
ALRIGHT, I'LL GET OUT OF YOUR HAIR.
YOU NEED TO REST
SORRY I WOKE YOU!
BETH AND LIZ WERE LEAVING AND I JUST DIDN'T WANT YOU TO WAKE UP WITH US ALL GONE
WAIT, WHAT?
BETH, SHE WAS HERE?
OF COURSE SHE WAS HERE!

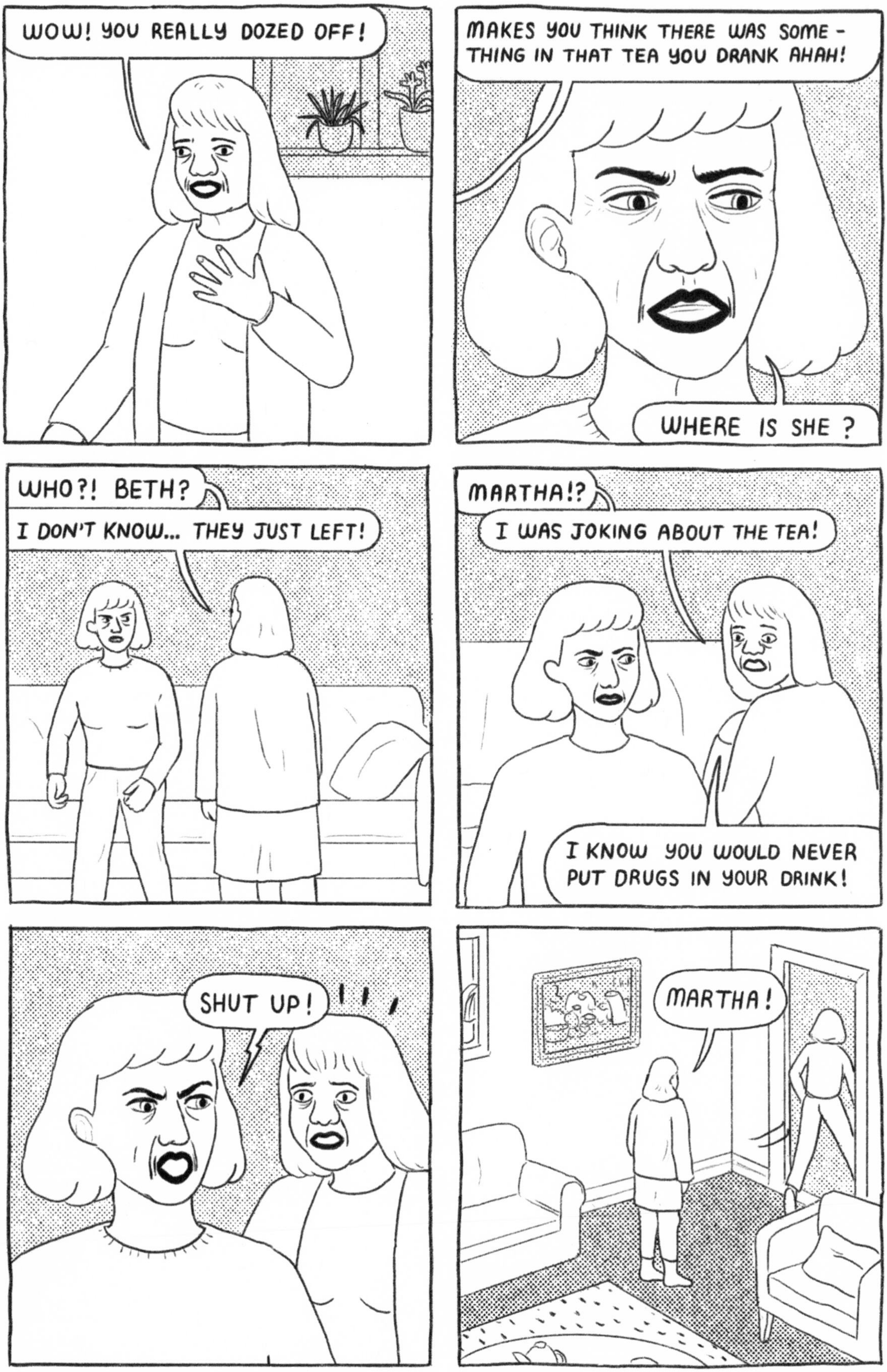
WOW! YOU REALLY DOZED OFF!
MAKES YOU THINK THERE WAS SOME-THING IN THAT TEA YOU DRANK AHAH!
WHERE IS SHE ?
WHO?! BETH?
I DON'T KNOW... THEY JUST LEFT!
MARTHA!?
I WAS JOKING ABOUT THE TEA!
I KNOW YOU WOULD NEVER PUT DRUGS IN YOUR DRINK!
SHUT UP!
MARTHA!

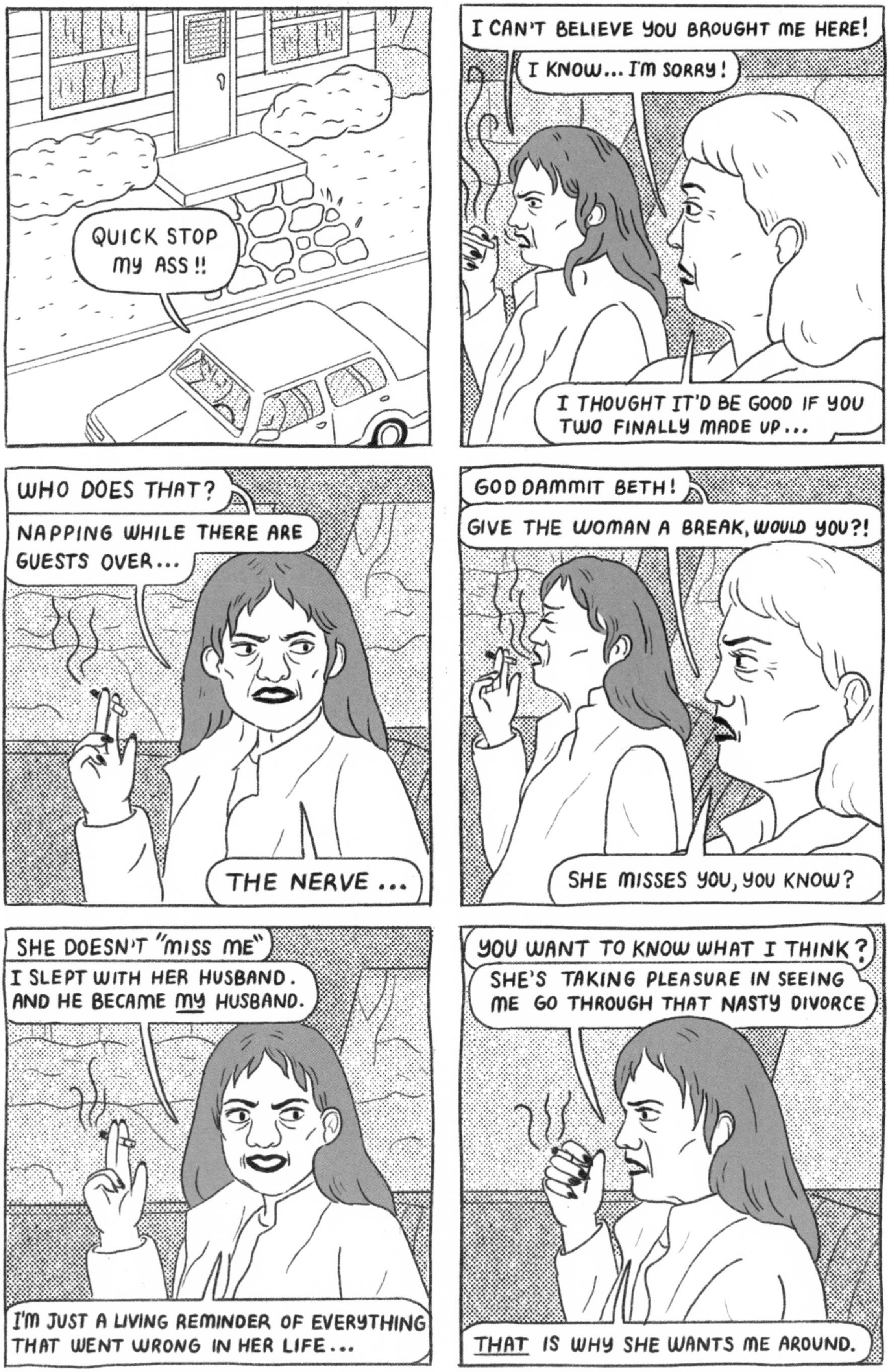
QUICK STOP MY ASS!!
I CAN'T BELIEVE YOU BROUGHT ME HERE!
I KNOW... I'M SORRY!
I THOUGHT IT'D BE GOOD IF YOU TWO FINALLY MADE UP...
WHO DOES THAT?
NAPPING WHILE THERE ARE GUESTS OVER...
THE NERVE...
GOD DAMMIT BETH!
GIVE THE WOMAN A BREAK, WOULD YOU?!
SHE MISSES YOU, YOU KNOW?
SHE DOESN'T "MISS ME"
I SLEPT WITH HER HUSBAND. AND HE BECAME MY HUSBAND.
I'M JUST A LIVING REMINDER OF EVERYTHING THAT WENT WRONG IN HER LIFE...
YOU WANT TO KNOW WHAT I THINK?
SHE'S TAKING PLEASURE IN SEEING ME GO THROUGH THAT NASTY DIVORCE
THAT IS WHY SHE WANTS ME AROUND.

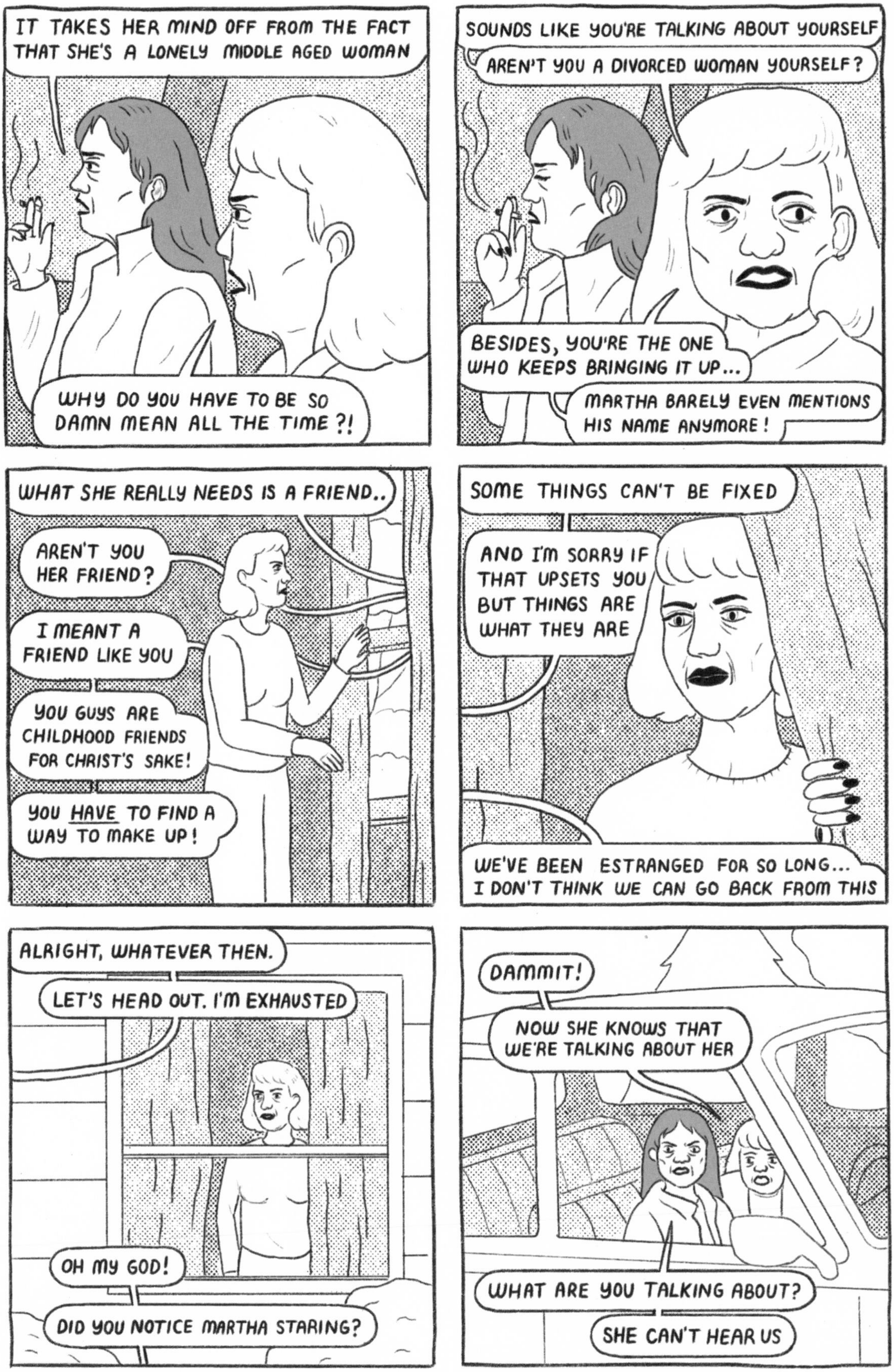
IT TAKES HER MIND OFF FROM THE FACT THAT SHE'S A LONELY MIDDLE AGED WOMAN
WHY DO YOU HAVE TO BE SO DAMN MEAN ALL THE TIME ?!
SOUNDS LIKE YOU'RE TALKING ABOUT YOURSELF
AREN'T YOU A DIVORCED WOMAN YOURSELF?
BESIDES, YOU'RE THE ONE WHO KEEPS BRINGING IT UP...
MARTHA BARELY EVEN MENTIONS HIS NAME ANYMORE!
WHAT SHE REALLY NEEDS IS A FRIEND..
AREN'T YOU HER FRIEND?
I MEANT A FRIEND LIKE YOU
YOU GUYS ARE CHILDHOOD FRIENDS FOR CHRIST'S SAKE!
YOU HAVE TO FIND A WAY TO MAKE UP!
SOME THINGS CAN'T BE FIXED
AND I'M SORRY IF THAT UPSETS YOU BUT THINGS ARE WHAT THEY ARE
WE'VE BEEN ESTRANGED FOR SO LONG... I DON'T THINK WE CAN GO BACK FROM THIS
ALRIGHT, WHATEVER THEN.
LET'S HEAD OUT. I'M EXHAUSTED
OH MY GOD!
DID YOU NOTICE MARTHA STARING?
DAMMIT!
NOW SHE KNOWS THAT WE'RE TALKING ABOUT HER
WHAT ARE YOU TALKING ABOUT?
SHE CAN'T HEAR US

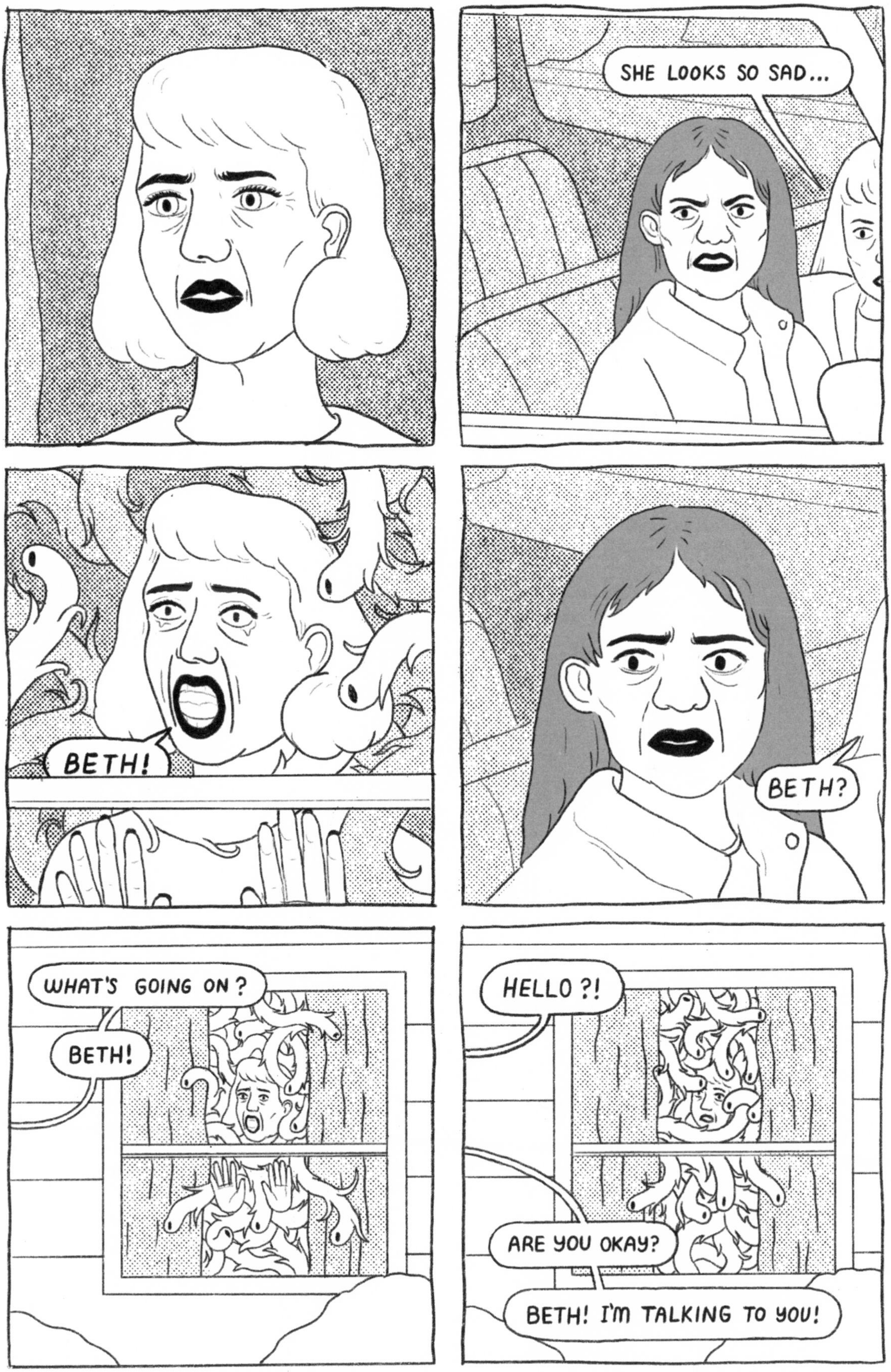
SHE LOOKS SO SAD...
BETH!
BETH?
WHAT'S GOING ON?
BETH!
HELLO?!
ARE YOU OKAY?
BETH! I'M TALKING TO YOU!

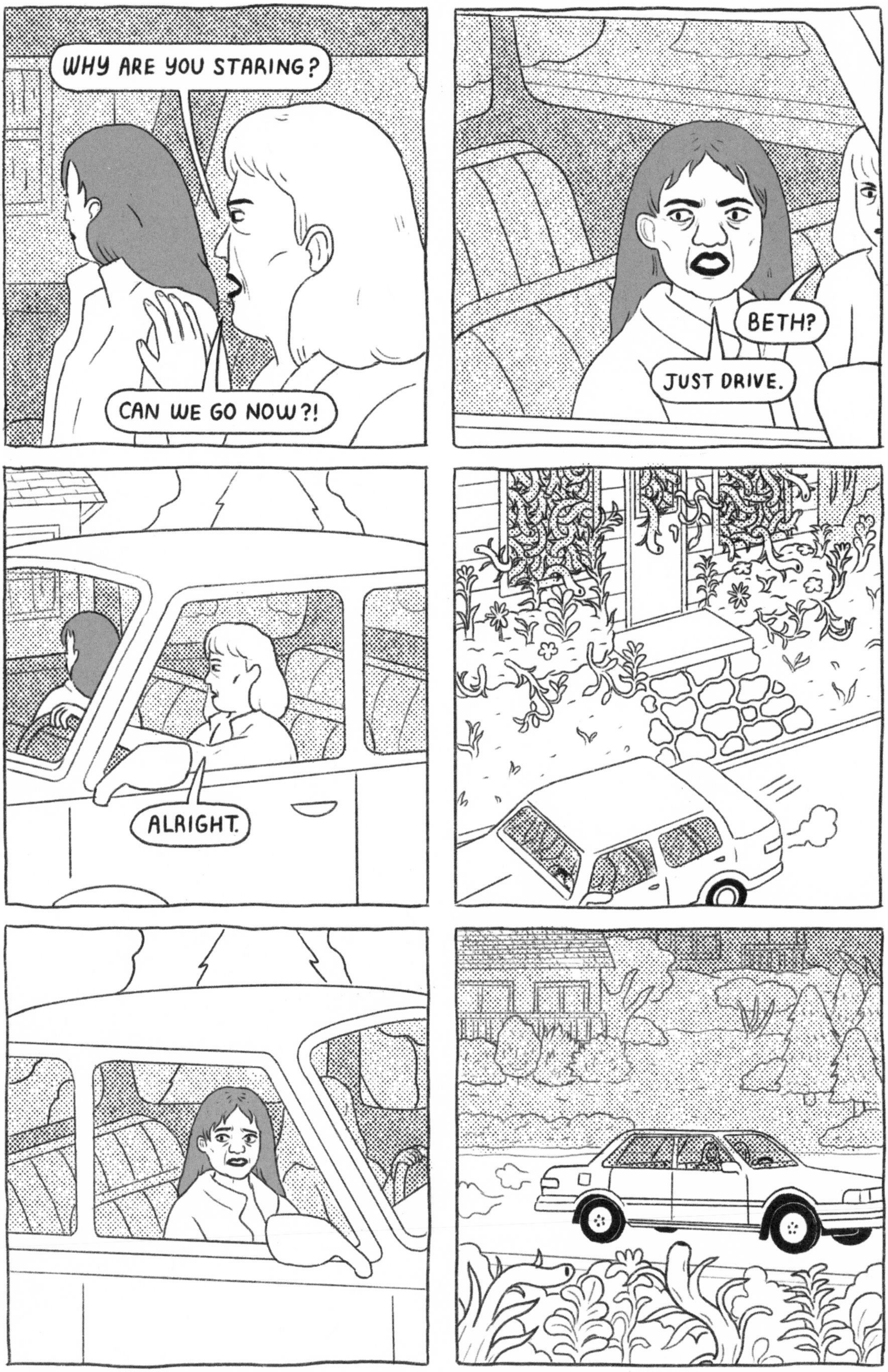
WHY ARE YOU STARING?
CAN WE GO NOW?!
BETH?
JUST DRIVE.
ALRIGHT.

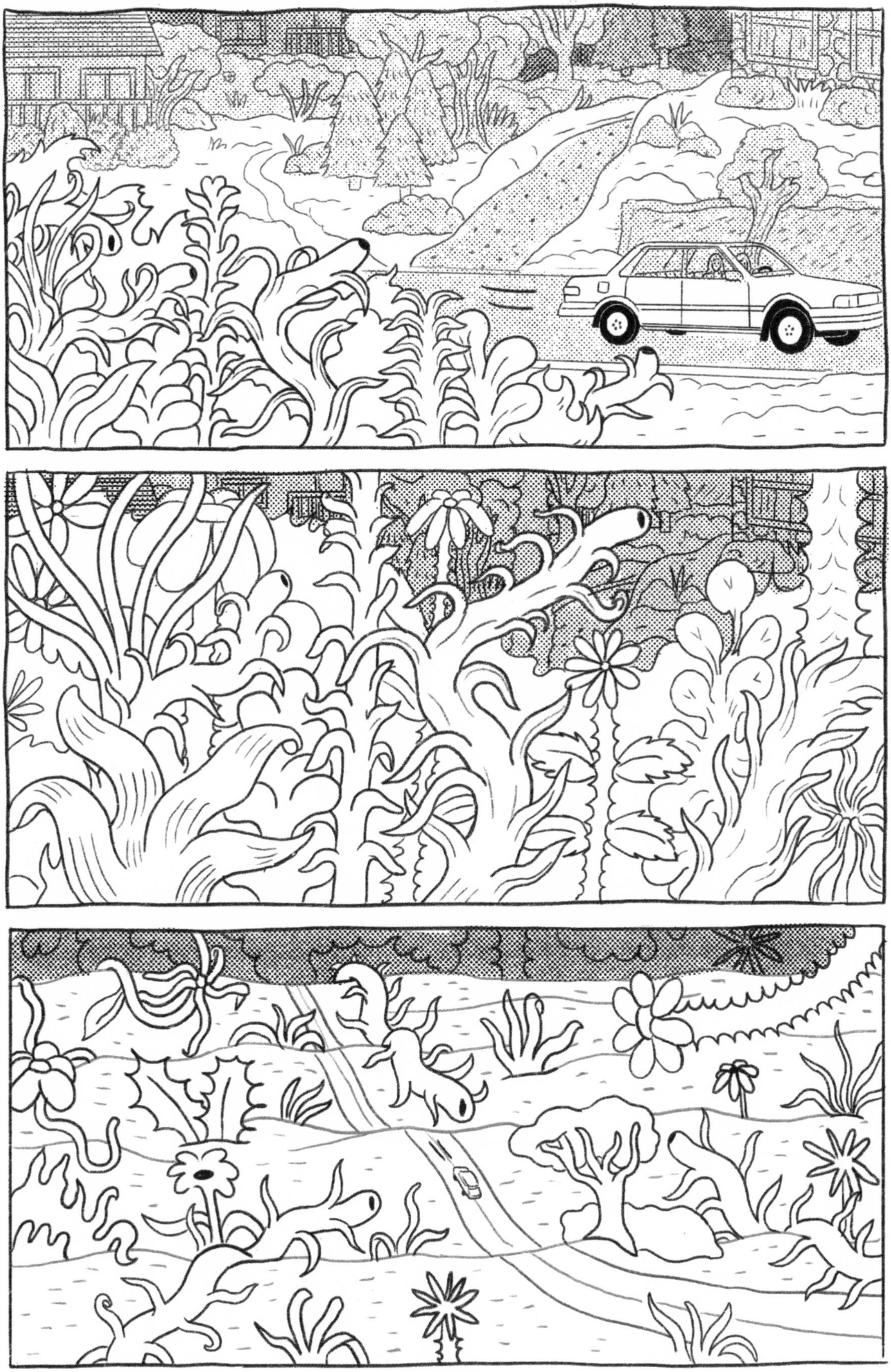

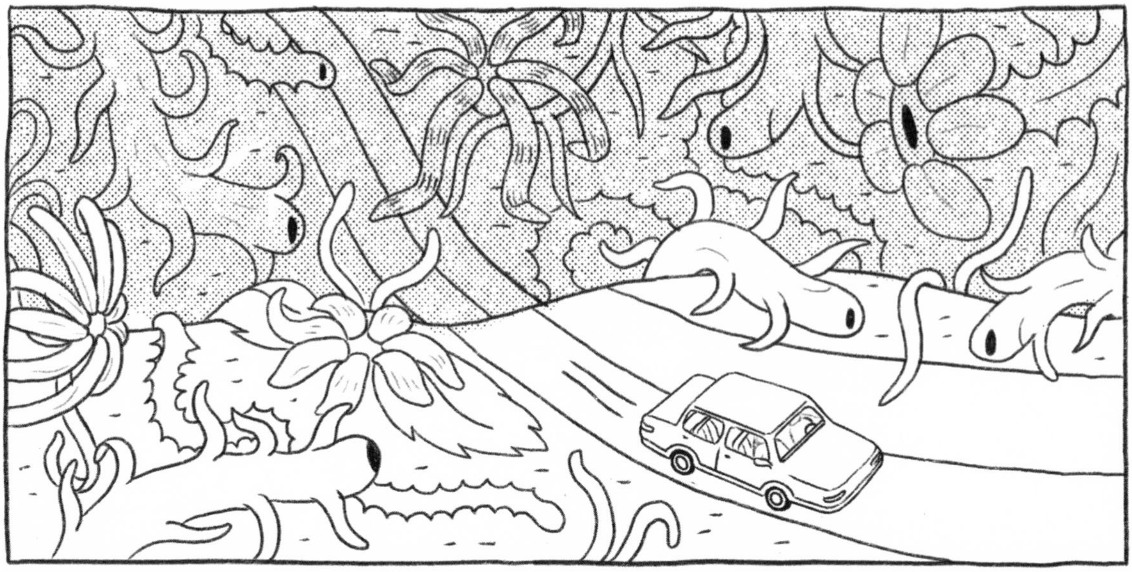

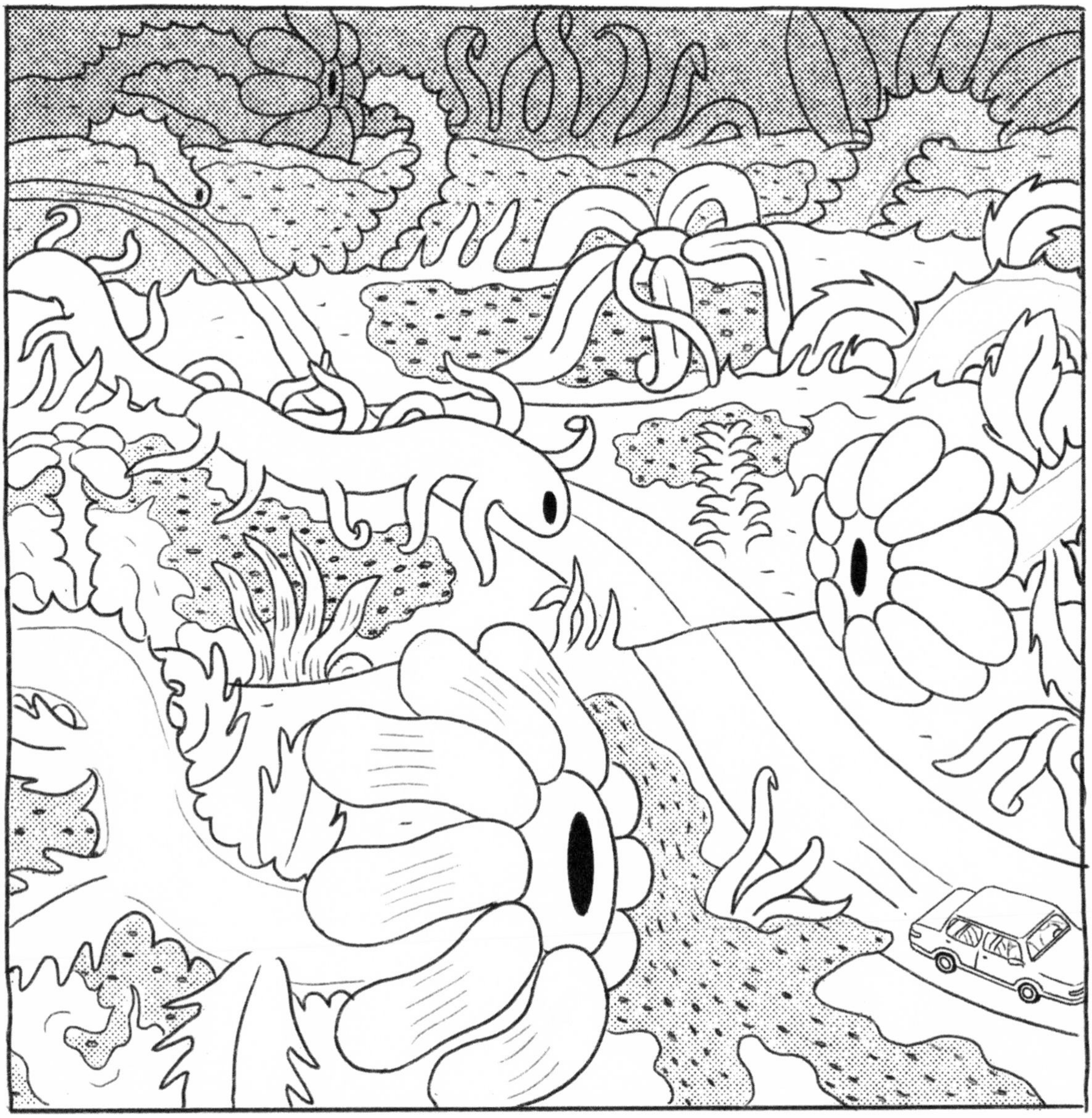

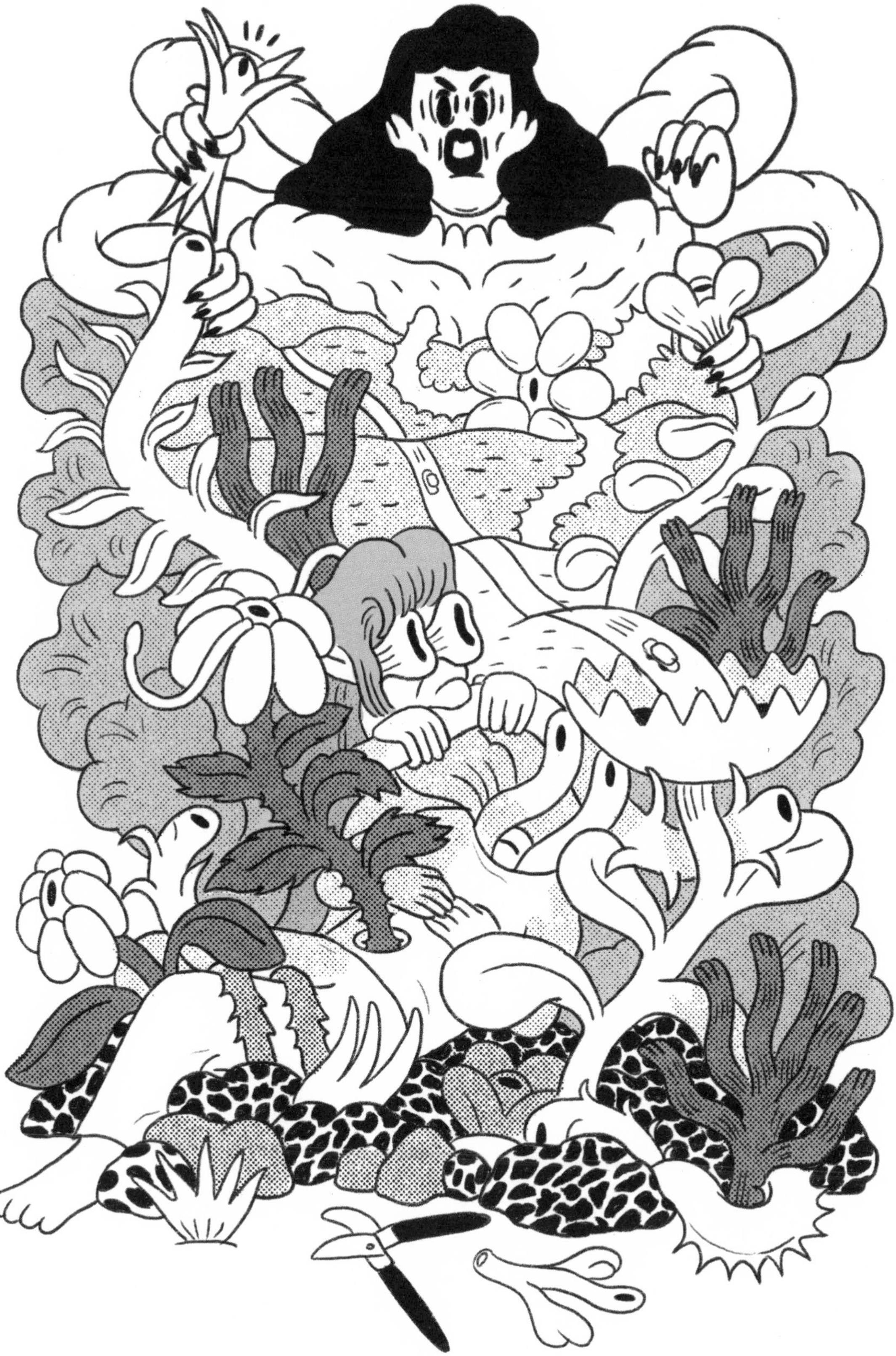

WEEDING

© 2021, GENEVIÈVE LEBLEU

FIRST EDITION

PRINTED BY GAUVIN IN QUEBEC, CANADA

LIBRARY DATA AVAILABLE FROM LIBRARY AND ARCHIVES CANADA UPON REQUEST

CONUNDRUM PRESS
WOLFVILLE, NS, CANADA
WWW.CONUNDRUMPRESS.COM

CONUNDRUM PRESS IS LOCATED IN MI'KMA'KI, THE ANCESTRAL TERRITORY OF THE MI'KMAK PEOPLE

THE PUBLISHER ACKNOWLEDGES THE FINANCIAL SUPPORT OF THE CANADA COUNCIL FOR THE ARTS, THE GOVERNMENT OF CANADA AND THE PROVINCE OF NOVA SCOTIA TOWARD THEIR PUBLISHING PROGRAM.

THE AUTHOR ACKNOWLEDGES THE FINANCIAL SUPPORT OF THE CANADA COUNCIL FOR THE ARTS AND THE CONSEIL DES ARTS ET LETTRES DU QUÉBEC TOWARD THE CREATION OF THIS WORK.

Canada Council
for the Arts

Conseil des Arts
du Canada

CALQ
Conseil
des arts
et des lettres
du Québec

NOVA SCOTIA

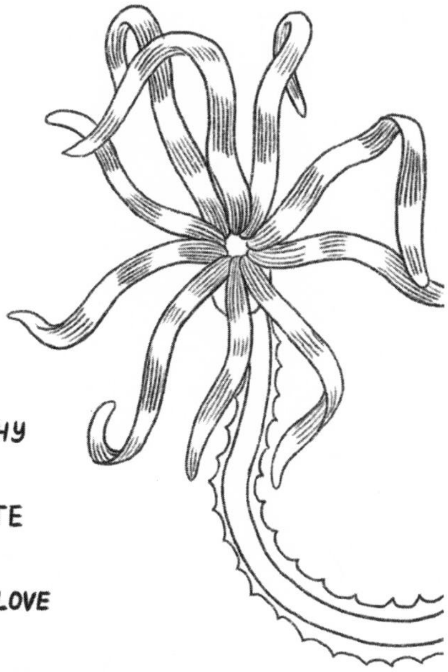

THANK YOU TO:

ANDY FOR YOUR PATIENCE AND EMPATHY

CARINE FOR BEING THE BEST STUDIOMATE

PHILIPPE FOR YOUR ENDLESS SUPPORT AND LOVE

MOM FOR LISTENING TO MY PROBLEMS AND CARING

PENELOPE AND CHLOË FOR YOUR UNCONDITIONAL FRIENDSHIP

ROBY AND VIRGINIE FOR YOUR GENERAL ENTHUSIASM TOWARDS MY ART

THOMAS FOR READING MY MANY DRAFTS AND COPY EDITING MY GRANT SUBMISSIONS

AND TO ANYONE WHO HAS EXPRESSED THEIR SUPPORT IN ANY SHAPE OR FORM:
I LOVE YOU AND I DID NOT FORGET YOU!

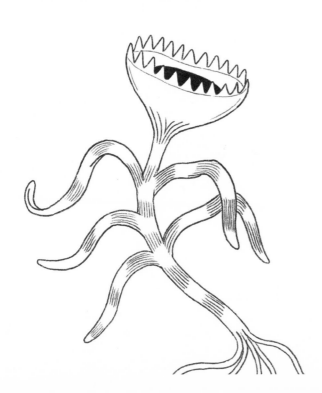